Unconventional Combat

Recent Titles In

OXFORD STUDIES IN CULTURE AND POLITICS

Clifford Bob and James M. Jasper, General Editors

Discursive Turns and Critical Junctures
Debating Citizenship after the Charlie Hebdo Attacks
Donatella della Porta, Pietro Castelli Gattinara, Konstantinos Eleftheriadis,
and Andrea Felicetti

Democracy Reloaded
Inside Spain's Political Laboratory from 15-M to Podemos
Cristina Flesher Fominaya

Public Characters
The Politics of Reputation and Blame
James M. Jasper, Michael P. Young, and Elke Zuern

Empire's Legacy
Roots of a Far-Right Affinity in Contemporary France
John W.P. Veugelers

Situational Breakdowns
Understanding Protest Violence and other Surprising Outcomes
Anne Nassauer

Democratic Practice
Origins of the Iberian Divide in Political Inclusion
Robert M. Fishman

Contentious Rituals
Parading the Nation in Northern Ireland
Jonathan S. Blake

Contradictions of Democracy
Vigilantism and Rights in Post-Apartheid South Africa
Nicholas Rush Smith

Plausible Legality
Legal Culture and Political Imperative in the Global War on Terror
Rebecca Sanders

Legacies and Memories in Movements
Justice and Democracy in Southern Europe
Donatella della Porta, Massimiliano Andretta, Tiago Fernandes
Eduardo Romanos, and Markos Vogiatzoglou

Taking Root
Human Rights and Public Opinion in the Global South
James Ron, Shannon Golden, David Crow, and Archana Pandya

Curated Stories
The Uses and Misuses of Storytelling
Sujatha Fernandes

The Human Right to Dominate
Nicola Perugini and Neve Gordon

Some Men
Feminist Allies and the Movement to End Violence Against Women
Michael A. Messner, Max A. Greenberg, and Tal Peretz

Unconventional Combat

*Intersectional Action in
the Veterans' Peace Movement*

MICHAEL A. MESSNER

OXFORD
UNIVERSITY PRESS

OXFORD

UNIVERSITY PRESS

Oxford University Press is a department of the University of Oxford. It furthers
the University's objective of excellence in research, scholarship, and education
by publishing worldwide. Oxford is a registered trade mark of Oxford University
Press in the UK and certain other countries.

Published in the United States of America by Oxford University Press
198 Madison Avenue, New York, NY 10016, United States of America.

© Oxford University Press 2021

Library of Congress Cataloging-in-Publication Data
Names: Messner, Michael A., author.
Title: Unconventional combat : intersectional action in the veterans'
peace movement / Michael A. Messner.
Description: New York, NY : Oxford University Press, [2021] |
Series: Oxford studies in culture and politics |
Includes bibliographical references and index.
Identifiers: LCCN 2020058608 (print) | LCCN 2020058609 (ebook) |
ISBN 9780197573631 (hardback) | ISBN 9780197573648 (paperback) |
ISBN 9780197573662 (epub)
Subjects: LCSH: Peace movements—United States—History—21st century. |
Veterans—Political activity—United States—History—21st century. |
Discrimination in the military—United States. | Harassment in the military—
United States. | Homophobia in the military—United States.
Classification: LCC JZ5584.U6 M47 2021 (print) | LCC JZ5584.U6 (ebook) |
DDC 303.6/6086970973—dc23
LC record available at https://lccn.loc.gov/2020058608
LC ebook record available at https://lccn.loc.gov/2020058609

DOI: 10.1093/oso/9780197573631.001.0001

1 3 5 7 9 8 6 4 2

Paperback printed by Marquis, Canada
Hardback printed by Bridgeport National Bindery, Inc., United States of America

Gratefully dedicated to the veterans I profile in this book, and to their generation of intersectional social justice activists.

Intergenerationality has always been an important dimension of sustainable radical movements. But the involvement of older people works, as these movements have emphasized, only if the elders refrain from assuming that they are in possession of the most relevant organizing knowledge. Moreover, international outreach is linked to an understanding of the intersectionality of struggles that insists on the leadership of those who have been previously marginalized. In many instances, this means that new organizations are led by young, Black, queer women who are intentionally challenging old leadership forms that accentuate individualism and charisma, and who are introducing new forms of leadership.

—Angela Y. Davis, 2020

Contents

List of Illustrations

Acknowledgments

Many thanks to all of the About Face and Veterans For Peace members who shared their stories with me. Special thanks and appreciation to the six veterans whose life histories form the centerpiece of my narrative; this book would not have been possible without the generous contributions of time and trust from Wendy Barranco, Phoenix Johnson, Monique Salhab, Monisha Ríos, Stephen Funk, and Brittany Ramos DeBarros. I also thank the members of the Joan Duffy chapter of Veterans for Peace in Santa Fe, New Mexico, Colleen Kelly and Shelley Rockett in the national VFP office, and Jovanni Reyes of About Face.

As I worked on this project, I was supported and encouraged by my colleagues and students in the departments of sociology and gender and sexuality studies at the University of Southern California. During my many years of immersion in sociology and gender studies, my understanding of the importance and power of intersectionality as political praxis was nurtured by reading and listening to the work of women of color, as it was deepened by longtime mentoring from Maxine Baca Zinn, and enhanced by conversations with younger scholar-activists, especially recent PhD students Chelsea Johnson and LaToya Council, who brought home to me the necessity of applying intersectionality in my own backyard.

As I conducted research for his book, I was assisted in various ways by Jae Kwon, Christine Williams, Martin Button, Daniel Craig, Joseph Hawkins, Maxine Baca Zinn, Raewyn Connell, Amber Train, Yael Findler, Stephanie Bonnes, and Dean Birkenkamp. The book was improved due to thoughtful readings of all or parts of the manuscript by Michelle Livings, James Jasper, Jeffrey Montez de Oca, Ken Mayers, Chelsea Johnson, Pierrette Hondagneu-Sotelo, and the anonymous readers at Oxford University Press. Warm gratitude to a dozen members of the Santa Fe and Albuquerque VFP chapters who invited me to present my ideas during the eleventh hour, as I was tying up the final draft of this book; their thoughts and comments in a Zoom conversation were extremely helpful in sharpening my argument. And many thanks to veteran and artist Aaron Hughes for creating the powerful cover art for the book, to my editor James Cook, and to all of the editorial and production staff at OUP.

Finally, my USC colleague and partner Pierrette Hondagneu-Sotelo has lived with this project, and with me, as I researched and wrote this book—from South Pasadena to Santa Fe, through learning to teach online, while enduring the COVID-19 pandemic, contributing to an exploding movement for racial justice, and through the joys and tribulations of puppy-raising. As always, my daily life with Pierrette has buoyed me, as her progressive scholarship and her generosity of spirit has inspired me.

Prologue

In her 1973 fable "The ones who walk away from Omelas," the writer Ursula K. Le Guin imagines a village, Omelas, where life is apparently perfect.[1] The air and water are clean, good food is abundant, all enjoy music, love, peace, and plenty. Children take their good fortune for granted—at least until they learn, as all must, that everyone's happiness and prosperity depend on maintaining the misery of one small child who is imprisoned in a tiny and filthy basement cell, with scant food, no medical care, and no human contact. Le Guin's story is often used in high school and college classes as a springboard for discussing how privilege works—how easy it is to turn a blind eye to the ways that our daily comforts are grounded in the exploitation or misery of unseen others. And the story poses a moral quandary for individuals: Do you accept the situation, enjoying the comforts and joys of daily life, or do you, like a few individuals in Le Guin's story, "walk away" from Omelas to some other imagined destination?

I recently used this story to launch a class on violence and social justice with first-year college students, and they deftly identified parallels between Le Guin's story and our own lives: Our enjoyment of out-of-season fresh fruits, provided at the expense of farmworkers who toil for low wages while facing health risks from pesticides; the privilege, even, of discussing this short story in a gleaming university, while poor kids just a few blocks from our campus struggle in under-funded schools. How, I pondered with my students, can one live an ethical life in such a context? One of my students challenged a premise of Le Guin's story, observing that "many of the big problems we face today are not ones that individuals can just 'walk away' from." What are these problems, I asked? Climate change, several said in unison. War, another said, especially nuclear war. Global pandemics, said another—and this was before the COVID-19 pandemic. It is certainly possible, we agreed—especially with a bit of lead-time—for the super-rich to insulate themselves from the ravages of climate change, wars, or pandemics. But the interconnectedness of these global challenges reveals individual escape as an impossible fantasy, and it also places nationalism in the spotlight as a consistently destructive source of these massive problems.

If we learn anything from the 2020 pandemic, the escalating climate change crisis, and the continuing militarization of the planet, it should be this: Consumer culture, coupled with the political climate of neoliberalism, may encourage us to think of ourselves as individual free agents navigating a world of personal choices, but in fact we are all intricately interconnected. Our individual biographies, to paraphrase the sociologist C. Wright Mills, are necessarily intertwined with history.[2] Escaping to a realm of individual freedom—"walking away from Omelas"—is an illusion. Instead, in the words of Simone de Beauvoir, "To will oneself free is also to will others free."[3]

Given the life and death challenges we face with climate change, escalating militarism, persistent racial and gender injustice, and the continuing scourge of global pandemics, are there ways that we can productively build interconnectedness—from local to global communities—that forges new directions toward lasting peace, social justice, and climate justice? It seems unlikely that the fresh ideas for radical realignments that we need will come from current corporate and governmental elites. As Naomi Klein argues, "shocks," such as wars, pandemics, or climate-caused catastrophes like massive hurricanes, droughts, and wildfires—too often trigger new waves of "disaster capitalism," as elites position themselves to privatize public institutions, militarize borders and cities, and further consolidate power and profit for themselves.[4] Instead, I argue in this book that we need to look to a new generation of social justice activists whose collective life experiences—struggling against race and class oppression, sexual violence, war and militarism—create shared understandings of the interconnectedness of the major challenges we face, collective knowledge from the grassroots that fuels fresh approaches to building coalitions that work for structural change.

Unconventional Combat centers on the lives, words and strategies of a group of "post-9/11" U.S. military veterans, most of them women of color, most queer-identified, who are rising as a new generation of activist leaders in movements working for peace and social justice. I point to how their shared situated knowledge fuels intersectional action that presents challenges and new possibilities for progressive social movements. Their collective experiences as multiply-marginalized people have led these veterans to see sexual violence, racial violence, or the violences of climate destruction, wars, and militarization not as discrete phenomena that require separate interventions. Instead, in the words of sociologist Patricia Hill Collins, violence is "a saturated site of intersectionality . . . a form of conceptual glue that enables racism, sexism, class exploitation and heterosexism to function as they do."[5] All of the veterans I introduce in this book have been harmed by violence; none seek to "walk away" from the social injustices that generated the violence they have survived. Instead, these activists lean in to the belly of the beast, together building broad coalitions to confront militarism, climate change, sexual violence, and injustice to immigrants, Black, Indigenous, and people of color, as they seek to steer history in new, more just, and peaceful directions.

why can't dems
evolve w/ VFP?   See p.

1

Action at intersections

Wars, militarization, and veterans' peace movements

Conjure in your mind the image of a soldier at war. Most likely you pictured a helmeted man wielding a rifle. Or imagine a military veteran. Again, I would guess that most people will picture a man. The equation of men, masculinity, military service, and war is sharply chiseled into our popular imagination. It is a central point of this book that this gendered assumption is a barrier to understanding the true costs of war and an impediment to addressing the myriad problems presented by war and its aftermath. The celebration of men's warrior masculinity, according to feminist scholar Cynthia Enloe, is foundational to the costly and destructive militarization of society, which she defines as "a step-by-step process by which a person or a thing gradually comes to be controlled by the military *or* it comes to depend for its well-being on militaristic ideas."[1] Peace movements throughout history, however, have insisted that nothing is pre-ordained, that it is possible for people to redirect social priorities and steer the world in more peaceful and just directions. "What has been militarized," Enloe asserts, "can be demilitarized."[2]

"Demilitarization," scholar and veteran Benjamin Schrader has noted, "is partly tied up with the unraveling of masculinity."[3] The veterans' peace and justice organizations that I focus on in this book, Veterans For Peace (VFP) and About Face, are currently engaged in just such an unraveling of gender—and, simultaneously, of race and generation—as they grapple with the de-centering of older, heterosexual White men veterans' stories and leadership. In *Unconventional Combat*, I examine the pitfalls and possibilities of this jarring process by centering on the stories, struggles, and strategies of a younger generation of women, people of color, and LGBTQ2S[4] veterans who have become active in these organizations in recent years. This diverse cohort of younger vets infuses activism against war and militarism with a collective understanding—a "situated knowledge"—of the interconnectedness of racial, gender, social class, and sexual oppression and violence. This new generation of activists deploys this intersectional knowledge to

Unconventional Combat. Michael A. Messner, Oxford University Press. © Oxford University Press 2021.
DOI: 10.1093/oso/9780197573631.003.0001

actually they again business is,(?) exactual as usual(!).

challenge business-as-usual within VFP and About Face, as they simultaneously navigate new directions in forging a broad coalition politics with other organizations.

The title of this chapter, "Action at Intersections," speaks to two meanings of the word "intersections." First, it hints at colloquial understandings of intersecting boulevards simultaneously as vibrant sites of creative and promising action, and as dangerous places of collision and conflict. Second, it speaks to a scholarly approach to studying social inequalities, "intersectionality," which insists on studying the simultaneity of race, ethnicity, social class, gender, and sexuality.[5] The current emergence of younger women, women of color and LGBTQ2S people in veterans' peace and justice organizations carries precisely this range of contradictory possibilities and complexities. Their "actions at intersections" hold the promise of deepening and broadening the work of these organizations, at a time of relative abeyance in the peace movement. But should these organizations fail to be open to the wrenching process of change entailed by this intervention, they may be doomed to becoming less relevant as their membership ages, shrinks, and dies.

Women, the military, and war

From popular culture to transnational diplomacy and scholarly research, women's experiences of war and militarism are routinely ignored or rendered as an afterthought. Feminist scholars like Carol Cohn, Cynthia Enloe, Catherine Lutz, Judith Stiehm, and others have long sought to crack this silence, arguing that when we center on women's experiences—as soldiers' wives or widows,[6] as mothers,[7] as sex workers around military bases,[8] as survivors of military rape,[9] as military nurses,[10] or as soldiers[11]—we unveil a deeper understanding of the costs of wars,[12] the militarization of everyday life, and the proliferation of U.S. military bases around the world.[13] These ideas gained some international traction with the United Nations Security Council's passage in 2000 of UNSC Resolution 1325, which aimed, in the words of scholars Robert Egnell and Mayesha Alam, to bring "global attention to the plight of women during armed conflict as well as the need to ensure their participation in peace and security processes."[14]

Women have a long history of serving in militaries—most frequently as nurses, medics, and support staff.[15] The United States boasts by far the world's most well-funded and powerful military, with a reach that spans the globe. And though the military is still dominated by men, women have increased in number and expanded the scope of their participation in recent decades. In 1973, when military conscription ended, women made up a scant 2% of active duty members of the military. Today, women constitute 16% of U.S. military active duty and 18% of reserve personnel.[16] Proportionately, women service members are even more diverse than their male counterparts: Roughly one-third of women service members are Black, and more than half (56%) identify as a racial minority and/or as ethnically Hispanic.[17]

Since President Barack Obama in 2013 lifted the ban on women serving in combat roles, growing numbers of women have served in central battle zones of Iraq and Afghanistan, absorbing an escalating share of physical and psychological injuries, including moral injury.[18] The concept of moral injury has been increasingly deployed in recent years to refer to internalized trauma, often manifested as shame, for participating in killing or harming others in times of war.[19] The high numbers of civilian deaths in recent U.S. wars Afghanistan and Iraq have been a continuing source of moral injury for returning U.S. troops, both men and women.[20] Research by anthropologist Hugh Gusterson, echoed in Sonia Kennebeck's powerful 2016 documentary film *National Bird*, shows how troops—both women and men—who operate and support the remote killings of civilians in the Middle East through drone warfare, often suffer the deep trauma of moral injury.[21]

An appalling proportion of the injury and trauma absorbed by military women is delivered not by foreign combatants, but by men from their own ranks. Recent research by sociologist Stephanie Bonnes concludes that "More than half of the women serving in the U.S. military have experienced workplace sexual harassment, with some estimates as high as 79%."[22] In a comprehensive 2018 study commissioned by the U.S. Marine Corps to answer the question, "What it is like to be both a woman and a marine," Rebecca Lane and her colleagues paint a picture of endemic sexual assault, hostile work environments, online sexual harassment, and officers who perceive women as weak and undeserving of being in the Corps.[23] Stalking experiences during military service, Carrie L. Lewis and her colleagues found, commonly causes PTSD and depression.[24] As a result, over half a million U.S. women veterans have enrolled in the Veterans Administration (VA) health care system, many of them seeking support for what Suzanne Gordon has called the "vexing problem" of military sexual trauma (MST).[25]

As a racially diverse cohort of women in the military has grown in recent decades, so too has the visibility of LGBTQ2S people in the service. Most of the U.S. military's history is a story of compulsory heterosexuality coupled with institutional denials or violent suppression of same-sex desire and actions. But the "coming out" ethos of the gay and lesbian liberation movement of the 1970s was echoed in calls to eliminate the military's anti-gay policies. Prominent members of the military brass stiffly opposed including gay and lesbian people in the service. In what Randy Shilts called a "last great frenzy of antigay hostility," the U.S. military by the start of the 1990s had accelerated its rate of soldiers being drummed out of the service for homosexuality.[26]

In 1994, the Clinton administration instituted "Don't Ask, Don't Tell" (DADT), which became the official policy governing gay, lesbian, and bisexual people in the military until its repeal in 2011. Billed as a compromise at the time, DADT barred the military from punishing or discharging someone who was closeted, but it allowed the discharge of individuals who openly stated they were gay or lesbian, or who were seen or known to have engaged in same-sex relationships.[27] The 2011 elimination of DATD created legal inclusion for LGBTQ2S people in the U.S. military. However, scholars Brandon Alford and Shawna Lee argue that this greater statutory inclusion "does not address a number of cultural or institutional inequities that continue to hinder full inclusion of sexual minority service members."[28] As the stories in this book illustrate, hostility to non-heterosexual people in the military, especially when combined with gendered racism, continues to create a toxic and punishing experience for LGBTQ2S service members.

Gender and peace movements

From women's leadership to demand a nuclear test ban treaty in the early 1960s, to the 1981–2000 Greenham Common (England) Women's Peace Camp, to mothers in many parts of the world mobilizing maternal language to oppose "men's wars," women have long constituted the heart and soul of modern international peace movements.[29] Women in the U.S. were important contributors to the anti-draft movement during the American War in Vietnam, and since 2002, Code Pink: Women For Peace has been one of the most consistently visible organizations working to end U.S. wars and occupations.

Men, however, have long dominated veterans' peace organizations. Given women's low numbers and historically marginal positions in the U.S. military, this is not surprising. But part of the reason for men's domination of veterans' peace organizations also lay in the narrow definitions of manhood they learned as boys—conceptions that were amplified, enforced, and celebrated during their time in the military. In the 1960s and 1970s, women constituted a tiny minority of the membership of Vietnam Veterans Against the War, an organization whose leaders often expressed masculinist styles of combative street activism. And since its inception, Veterans For Peace has been dominated by men veterans (albeit with significant participation from "associate members," non-veterans, among whom women are a sizable number). This has begun to change. Women, women of color, and LGBTQ2S people are a growing proportion of "Post 9/11 veterans"—a term used to describe those who served in the military during the explosion of U.S. wars in the Middle East. This diverse cohort of veterans has begun to play larger and more visible roles in movements for peace and social justice, including contesting for leadership in VFP, and recently assuming many of the leadership positions in About Face.[30] But up until very recently, this increasing membership diversity has emerged during a time of waning activism and public visibility of VFP and About Face, and also of the larger peace movement.

It is instructive to examine the ebb and flow of veterans' peace and justice activism in light of the history of other progressive movements. In an influential book on the history of the U.S. women's movement, Leila Rupp and Verta Taylor described the work of women's rights activists between 1945 and the early 1960s as "survival in the doldrums." Contrary to popular belief, the women's movement had not died during that time of anti-feminist backlash, Rupp and Taylor argue. Rather, during those years of women's movement abeyance, continuing feminist activism, much of it under the public radar, helped to ensure "social movement continuity" that was the foundation for a new burst of feminism starting in the late 1960s.[31] So too, stretching from the Obama years and into the first years of the Trump presidency, the U.S. peace movement in general, and the veterans' peace movement in particular, largely receded from public view. A core of activist members persisted, however, with local efforts such as the weekly VFP peace vigil on a busy street corner in Santa Fe, NM, that I regularly join, to About Face's traveling national "Drop the MIC" campaign to educate the public about the economic and human costs of the Military Industrial Complex.

There is much at stake in this challenge from a younger and more diverse group of veterans, not the least of which is the long-term survival of VFP. From a dwindling membership of perhaps 800 people in 2001, VFP membership mushroomed to roughly 10,000 members in 2005–2006, during the height of the Bush-Cheney escalation of wars in Afghanistan and Iraq.[32] But by 2020 VFP had settled back to an organization of a bit more than 3,000 members, disproportionately older White men of the Vietnam War generation. At the 2004 national VFP convention, younger veterans freshly returned from the conflicts in the Middle East gestated Iraq Veterans Against the War. Over the next few years, IVAW grew rapidly into a visible presence in the anti-war movement.[33] A decade later, IVAW changed its name to About Face: Veterans Against the War, in order to be inclusive of all "Post 9/11" vets, and also possibly to counter the recent trending-down of the organization's membership numbers and public visibility. In interviews I conducted for this book, activists—older and younger alike—openly addressed the question of whether or not VFP and/or About Face would survive as organizations. Also at stake, assuming they do survive, is just *how* VFP and About Face will do their work, both internally as organizations with increasingly diverse memberships, and externally in bridging toward coalitions with other national and international peace and justice organizations. In *Unconventional Combat*, I examine the strains, tensions, and possibilities of this historical moment through the lens of intersectionality.

Intersectionality and political praxis

In her groundbreaking 1990 book, *Black Feminist Thought*, Patricia Hill Collins challenged the foundations of how we think about social theory.[34] Rather than simply receiving theory as a legacy of great ideas handed down from the past by great (mostly White, Euro-American) men, Collins argued that our understandings of the world, including how to change it, can be deepened by viewing theory as emanating from the ground up, through the shared experiences and collective knowledge of oppressed peoples. The idea that collective knowledge of people from the bottom rungs of society can generate critical theory and transformative action—praxis—is not new. Karl Marx argued that industrial working-class peoples' experiences of alienation and exploitation in capitalist labor relations could develop into revolutionary class-based praxis.[35] In the late 1960s and early 1970s, the Brazilian educator Paulo Freire created a critical pedagogy through which peasants drew from their own situated knowledge to forge a liberatory anti-colonial praxis.[36] And the sociologist Dorothy Smith developed a standpoint theory of gender, to explain how women's everyday experiences of gender oppression, including unpaid, under-paid, and under-valued "women's work," can fuel anti-patriarchal praxis.[37] The radical core of Patricia Hill Collins's contribution is her insistence on never reducing critical praxis to a single aspect of experience and identity. Race, ethnicity, gender, social class, and sexuality are simultaneously always there in individual identities, group interactions, and social institutions.[38] And since people are differently located within institutional matrixes of domination, their experiences differ accordingly, as does the knowledge that is produced in those social locations.

We should never overstate or trivialize the idea of situated knowledge—for instance, assuming that a multiply-marginalized individual will necessarily have access to some over-arching superior "truth." But the most general implication of Collins's theory of knowledge is that *groups of people*—like Black women, colonized and racially marginalized people, poor working-class and LGBTQ2S people—who are situated in social positions of oppression, are likely to share experiences that can become resources for shaping critical understandings of the workings of power. Those in positions of privilege also share situated knowledge with each other. "Whiteness," sociologist Robin DiAngelo argues, "is a standpoint . . . that shapes our perspectives, experiences and responses."[39] So does being a man, being wealthy, being heterosexual, or being a citizen of a rich and powerful nation. But those of us who experience the world from positions of privilege are less likely to "see" the multiple workings of oppression, unless and until we learn to listen to, and view the world through, the stories of oppressed others. It follows, too, that privileged peoples' progressive praxis should be guided by the analysis and leadership of multiply-marginalized peoples.

Patricia Hill Collins's work has helped to create one of the most important developments in the social sciences in recent decades. The coining of the term "intersectionality" is correctly credited to legal studies scholar Kimberlee Crenshaw,[40] but as political scientist Ange-Marie Hancock points out in her 2016 book, *Intersectionality: An Intellectual History*, the roots of the ideas systematized by Crenshaw, Collins, and others in the 1980s and 1990s have a long history in the writings of women of color.[41] Here, rather than reviewing the history and the rich internal debates in the field, I want to focus on two dimensions of intersectionality that are germane to my study. First, the analytic lens of intersectionality sharpens our understanding of how multiple experiences of race-class-gender-sexual oppression shape socially situated identities, within institutions that are themselves structured by a matrix of domination. Perhaps nobody articulated the personal experience of being located at the nexus of multiple systems of oppression more succinctly than the writer Audre Lorde, who in a widely reproduced 1980 speech, said, "As a forty-nine-year-old Black lesbian feminist socialist mother of two, including one boy, and a member of an interracial couple, I usually find myself a part of some group defined as other, deviant, inferior, or just plain wrong."[42] In *Unconventional Combat*, I place at the center of my analysis the stories of six veterans whose experiences of multiple marginalization echo those of Lorde.

Second, increasingly today, intersectionality is emerging not simply as an academic theory, method, or field, but also as a radical praxis in social movements, a way of simultaneously understanding and acting to change the world.[43] Again, I take inspiration from Patricia Hill Collins, who in her 2019 book on this topic, zeroes in on the ways that intersectionality, as a critical theory, "sits in a sweet spot between critical analysis and social action."[44] I intend *Unconventional Combat* to illuminate this "sweet spot" through an examination of military veterans' movements for peace and social justice.

Intersectionality and veterans' peace movements

Thirty years ago, scholar-activist Barbara Omolade lamented, "The peace movement suffers greatly from its lack of a historical and holistic perspective, practice, and vision that include the voices and experiences of people of color; the movement's goals and messages have therefore been easily coopted and expropriated by world leaders who share the same culture of racial dominance and arrogance."[45] In recent years, younger activists—many of them women, people of color, and LGBTQ2S "millennials"—are growing in number and increasingly contesting for leadership positions in a wide range of progressive social movements.[46] The veterans who are my focus in *Unconventional Combat* are a part of what sociologist Ruth Milkman has dubbed a "new political generation" of movement activists who are racially and sexually diverse, and tend to view their work through the lens of intersectionality.[47]

A key element of intersectional movement activism involves coalition-building across what might otherwise be viewed as separate or even competing "causes." Indeed, sociologist Veronica Terriquez found a great deal of "intersectional mobilization" and "social movement spillover" among young queer activists and immigrant rights activists, two progressive efforts that, until recently, might have operated on entirely separate activist tracks.[48] Similarly, sociologist Heather McKee Hurwitz observes evidence of "feminist spillover" into Black Lives Matter, a racial justice movement that "sought to include Black women's experiences in the movement and disrupt gender conflict when it has taken the form of male-dominated or gender-blind activism.[49] Sociologist Jo Reger, who studied the massive 2017 "Women's March" that formed in protest of Donald Trump's election, observed that part of the success of this and subsequent annual Women's Marches was the use of intersectionality as "a mobilization tool" to build broad alliances across groups and issues.[50]

This is not to say that millennial activists have solved the puzzles and tensions in building social inclusion and diversity. At the first Women's March in 2017, for instance, a huge number of women marchers donned pink "pussy hats" as an omnipresent symbol of resistance against Trump's "grab her by the pussy" boasting. Pussy hats and slogans like "This pussy bites back" were seen by many protestors as clever ways to appropriate powerful men's sexist comments and turn them into symbols of resistance. But some women of color argued that White women's celebratory adoption of the pussy hats was an expression of race privilege that ignored the reality that women of color must contend not just with sexism, but with gendered racism, including what Patricia Hill Collins has called "controlling images" of Black women as animalistic, hypersexual "Jezebels."[51] In fact, as sociologist Fatima Suarez observed, the 2017 Women's March in Los Angeles was criticized by women of color and transwomen for its lack of inclusiveness. Some women of color, she observed, were told that they were being " 'divisive' for raising issues such as race, class, and immigration."[52] At the substantially smaller 2020 Los Angeles Women's March, I observed that the speakers at the start of the march were nearly all women of color, representing various community organizations. I also observed far fewer "pussy hats"[53] than I saw in the 2017 March, and I saw a good number of signs and slogans about intersectionality, including one carried by a diverse group of young women (one of them a Black veteran) that read, "IF YOUR FEMINISM ISN'T INTERSECTIONAL, IT'S TRASH!" (Figure 1.1).

Clearly, intersectionality is "on the ground" among younger social movement activists, but it has yet to gain the high ground in many movement

Figure 1.1 Intersectionality on the ground at the 2020 Women's March, Los Angeles, CA
Photo by author

organizations. Younger activists frequently criticize older movement leaders for continuing to steer their organizations along single-identity, single-issue tracks—women's rights, or peace, or racial justice, or climate activism, for instance. By contrast, younger activists of color and LGBTQ2S activists seek to work within and among organizations that honor and benefit from their intersectional life experiences, identities, and knowledge.[54] Indeed, younger activists in VFP and About Face tell me that they are frequently frustrated with older members who see gender and sexual issues, including military sexual trauma, as "distracting," as diverting the organization's focus from its central "mission" to oppose militarization and promote peace.

Younger activists' claims that older movement leaders lack an intersectional perspective is frequently on the mark, but it can also be stark to the point of caricature. In fact, progressive activists have long seen the importance and necessity of building a diverse movement and of bridging their organizations to coalitions in communities, in the nation, and internationally. The older membership of VFP—predominantly White men—is a generational cohort of committed radical activists. As I show in my book *Guys Like Me*, these men have worked for all or much of their adult lives to build a movement for peace and justice.[55] They recognize the necessity to recruit younger veterans and to diversify their membership and leadership. After all, these are committed activists with deep roots in the peace movement and in the political left; 2020 is surely not the first time these men were pushed to confront race, gender, and sexual inequality in their own organization. Their generation of progressive activists has understood, at least theoretically, that war and militarism are interconnected with colonialism, capitalism, racism, sexism, and environmental destruction.

But a theoretical understanding of the interconnectedness of issues and oppressions does not always translate cleanly into intersectional action. A prime example is the women's movement of the 1960s through the 1980s, often criticized by women of color and lesbians for basing its "sisterhood is powerful" rhetoric, strategies, and goals on the falsely universalized experiences of White, middle-class, heterosexual women, thus ignoring the particular and often dire needs of poor or working-class women, lesbians, Indigenous women, or women of color.[56] However, a glance at table of contents of *Sisterhood Is Powerful*, the veritable bible of the revitalized women's movement, compiled by Robin Morgan in 1970, reveals a more complicated picture.[57] The book includes articles by and about a wide range of women, including poor women, secretarial workers, Black women, Chicanas, Native American women, Chinese women, witches, mothers, lesbians, military women, and on and on. But this impressive diversity does not mean that those who criticized the women's liberation movement's class and race bias were wrong. The form of "inclusiveness" seen in Morgan's anthology, however sincere, is more of stitched-together patchwork than a coherent prism that shows connections between different forms of oppression, connections that would be useful for building a movement that aims to confront sexism as it intersects with other forms of oppression.[58]

Like many feminists of the 1960s and 1970s, White women and men progressives working today in the veterans' peace movement routinely see the need for "diversity," but their efforts frequently fall short of opening space for the sorts of ideas and strategies that a newer, more diverse generation of activists bring to the struggle. The psychologist Ronni Michelle Greenwood provides a useful framework for thinking about the generational differences I analyze here. She observes that racially diverse cohorts of activists tend to express an "intersectional political consciousness" that too often clashes with what she calls a "consciousness of singularity" among less diverse activists who organize around "intragroup similarities arising from a shared social identity, such as gender."[59] Similarly, the older White male VFP members I have studied might see "anti-war veteran" as their "singular" shared movement identity, as their "master status," that brought them to VFP in the first place. By contrast, newer arrivals to VFP and About Face might see themselves not just as anti-war veterans, but also as women veterans, or women-of-color veterans, as queer black veterans, or Indigenous women veterans.

Some older men veterans' "consciousness of singularity" is understandable; becoming anti-war veterans is what brought these men together in the first place. But this singular identity as anti-war veterans can also veil the extent to which they share other identities—as men, as White, as heterosexual—that help to form the bonds between them, and create boundaries around them. It can also shape their orientations toward activism in ways that retain a narrow focus on the anti-war "mission" of the organization, while questioning whether connections with other issues—like confronting military sexual trauma, for instance—might be "distractions" that will dilute their activist focus. The older men in Veterans For Peace I have observed and interviewed seem sincerely committed to recruiting women and people of color to VFP. But their efforts to build diversity in the organization too often fall short. These failures are usually not due to bad faith. Rather, their shared situated knowledge, grounded in their experiences as (mostly) White, heterosexual men—including their years of service in almost entirely all-male military contexts that marginalized and disparaged women and punished non-heterosexual or feminine-presenting men—is a woefully insufficient knowledge-basis for creating intersectional praxis in a social movement.

The younger cohort of activist veterans I focus on in this book carry to their peace and justice work a commitment to intersectionality that is organically grounded in their shared, situated knowledge of the interconnectedness of race, gender, class, and sexual oppressions.[60] *Unconventional Combat* illuminates how this younger, more diverse cohort of veterans develops peace and justice strategies that logically flow from their collective experiential knowledge of violence and marginality in race, colonial, gender, social class and/or sexual relations during their youth and during their military service. Through their collective intersectional praxis, they are challenging established modes of movement-building by simultaneously seeking to upend traditional modes of White male leadership within these organizations, while also forging anti-racist and decolonizing bridges with other national and international peace and justice organizations.

The research

Unconventional Combat is based on a mix of research methods. Over the past few years, and starting with the research that I conducted for *Guys Like Me: Five Wars, Five Veterans for Peace*, I have been connected as a participant-observer with Veterans For Peace. I attended the national VFP conventions in 2017 and 2019, and participated in VFP's 2020 convention, which was conducted online due to the COVID-19 pandemic. Since 2016, I have participated as a member of the Santa Fe, NM, chapter of VFP, joining them on scores of Fridays at their weekly peace vigil, attending numerous local chapter meetings, marching with VFP in three Armistice Day ("Veterans Day") parades, and demonstrating with them in support of local youth climate-change activists. My connections with About Face are more recent, and thinner. I had intended to engage in some participant observation with About Face in 2020, but their public activities were short-circuited by the COVID-19 epidemic. About Face pivoted quickly during the quarantine period to hold numerous online forums on militarism and war, and their members participated in several online "town hall" forums, several of which I attended virtually in the spring and summer of 2020.

Participant observation with both of these organizations was invaluable for me to build an understanding of VFP's and About Face's internal organizational dynamics, and the organizations' debates and strategies for building coalitions in the larger social movements landscape. The book's narrative, though, rests heavily on interviews, especially the life history interviews that I conducted with a diverse group of six younger veterans who are active in Veterans For Peace and/or About Face. I also conducted fifteen shorter interviews with VFP and About Face members, most of them older White men, and the research was deepened through a number of brief, informal conversations I have had with members of these two organizations.

This book rests its analysis on the idea that groups of people develop "situated knowledge" grounded in their socially located experiences in systems of race, social class, gender, and sexual inequality. An obvious question, then, that any wise reader would ask concerns how my own situated knowledge might affect the stories and analysis that I develop here. I am not a veteran, for one thing. And I am an older, White, heterosexually-identified man who enjoys financial security as a tenured professor in a major research university. How has this social location of privilege shaped my knowledge? What might I miss, or perhaps distort the meanings of, in listening to life histories of people from very different backgrounds who are sharing stories with me about their experiences of sexual assault, gendered racism, homophobia, or the trauma of war? I can't confidently deliver clear answers to these questions, but I do include a short essay at the end of the book, Appendix I, that I intend as a more detailed window into my research process and some strategies I deploy to remain as reflexive as possible, while conducting research, analysis of data, and writing.

Organization of the book

In *Unconventional Combat*, I experiment with "Interludes" placed between chapters, which offer the reader brief snapshots taken from interviews or from participant observation of VFP or About Face events.[61] Interlude 1, which follows this introductory chapter, offers glimpses of VFP and About Face men's memories of women during their military careers, as a way of hinting at how their situated knowledge shapes their understandings or assumptions about gender, as veterans. Chapter 2 zeroes in close-up on the stories of six younger veterans—three of them women, all of them people of color, three of them queer-identified, one genderqueer nonbinary person, and one identified as an Indigenous Two-Spirit person. Drawing on life history interviews with these six veterans, I trace how their experiences with racism, sexism, homophobia, and gender/sexual violence during their youth and during their military careers shapes the situated knowledge they bring to peace and justice activism.

Interlude 2 presents a field note I recorded at the 2019 VFP convention, an observation of an informal moment in a hotel elevator, when older White VFP men joked with each other about inviting some young Asian women flight attendants to their rooms. In Chapter 3, I describe an electric moment of group debate and conflict about gender, race, and coalition politics at the 2019 VFP convention's business meeting. I use this moment as a point of departure to analyze the often-painful clash between the older generation's efforts to build organizational "diversity" with the younger veterans' more expansive intersectionality. Here, I zero in on the organizational processes in

VFP and About Face that serve to limit, marginalize, or in some cases expand the full participation of this new generation.

Interlude 3 presents a lightly edited transcript of a June 2020 podcast interview with VFP member Monique Salhab, who speaks about militarized police and racist violence, during the height of the COVID pandemic and the national uprisings over the police murder of George Floyd in Minneapolis. Chapter 4 turns outward, examining the ways that VFP and About Face attempt to forge coalitions within the broader national and international peace movement, and with organizations working for climate justice, for decolonization and justice for Indigenous people, and ending racial, gender, and sexual violence. The contribution of the younger generation of activists, I will show, is not that they have invented coalition-building, but that they bring an intersectional orientation to *how* to build bridges and forge coalitions within the larger ecology of movement organizations.

Interlude 4, a field note from the Veterans For Peace 2020 national convention, spotlights the congruences and tensions between Indigenous decolonial efforts and progressive anti-militarism. In the final chapter, I draw from my observations and interviews to consider the future of VFP and About Face within the larger field of national and international movements for peace and social justice. I end by highlighting how the intersectional praxis of a new generation of progressive activists holds the promise of bridging the struggle against militarism and war with other large issues of the day, including climate change, global pandemics, and the continuing violence of economic, racial, gender, and sexual injustice.

Interlude 1
"It was all men"

In my interviews with men members of Veterans For Peace and/or About Face in 2019 and 2020, I asked, **"When you were in the military, what kinds of interactions did you have with women?"**

Well, there might have been some enlisted women. There were no women officers as far as I know. There were nurses. But those would have been the only ones I was ever exposed to. So, the women aspect of the military, was completely not there.

—Joe, 87-year-old White air force veteran

When I was serving, there were very, very few women marines. And I have to admit that women marines were not treated with much respect in those days. They were referred to as BAMs: B-A-M, which stood for Broad-Assed-Marines. Once I left Quantico, I don't think I ever encountered another woman marine in eight and a half years.

—Vic, 82-year-old White marine corps veteran

Women? There were no women when I was in the service.

—Steven, 74-year-old White army veteran

In boot camp women didn't exist. I don't remember ever seeing a woman. Zero. Even later in Germany. Women in the military—I'm trying to think if I saw any. There must have been but I just fail to recall. We would try to go out to the German clubs and meet German women, but women were not part of my experience at all, as military.

—Mac, 73-year-old White army veteran

It's all male. The artillery battalions, like 120 personnel, all male. There were women in support unit stuff—medical supply, logistic stuff, some office clerical type stuff, but not in our battalion. There was no slots for female soldiers. It was all men.

—Santiago, 57-year-old Latino army veteran

There was no women in the infantry. There would be women working up the hill, like officers.

—Hiram, 44-year-old White army veteran

I was in the marines. My MOS was landing support, and there were women, some in my training. That was the only time I ever interacted with women really was during my MOS school.

—Douglas, 37-year-old Asian American marine corps veteran

My experience with women in the National Guard was very little, very few, and far between. Most of the companies were infantry, so they were all men at the time. We did interact with female soldiers: sometimes they would be serving in the mess hall, serving food, or sometimes as part of military custodial services, and for the administrative things on base, like intake or out-take for medical services for recruits.

—Lewis, 34-year-old African American National Guard veteran

2

"I was in unconventional combat"

Intersectional pathways through the military

The United States ended its army draft in 1973. Almost immediately, people began to worry about the future of the U.S. military: If young people are no longer conscripted into military service, who will enlist? In subsequent decades, a large part of the answer to that question lay in the affinity between, on the one hand, the masculinist structure and values of the military, and on the other hand, the developing masculine identities of boys and young men who, during their formative years, had been steeped in a culture of militarized patriotic heroism in their families, communities, and popular culture. In the years and decades after the draft was eliminated, "a few good men" (to draw from a mid-1980s marine corps recruiting slogan), have continued to gravitate to the military.

But the men who join the military are not drawn evenly from all social strata: social class, education, race, and geography are important factors in shaping who enlists. Military recruiters know this, focusing their pitches to boys in working-class and poor families and schools, particularly in small towns and urban areas disproportionately populated by people of color. Consequently, as many critics have pointed out, it is more accurate to say that the "all volunteer" U.S. military is populated not so much through an accumulation of individual free choices, but rather, through an "economic draft," that is also in many ways a "racial draft."

Take a generation of boys—especially those in rural small towns or poor urban areas that offer few avenues to higher education, gainful employment, or economic mobility. Engage these boys in fantasy warrior play, and immerse them in video games, TV and movie images that glorify war as sites for the enactment of manly patriotic heroism. Teach them to revere the older men around them who served in their country's military. And promise them that their own service will be rewarded with similar respect, as well as education and training for future careers. By the time they are in their late teens, many such young men—like Gulf War veteran Daniel Craig, whom I profiled

Unconventional Combat. Michael A. Messner, Oxford University Press. © Oxford University Press 2021.
DOI: 10.1093/oso/9780197573631.003.0002

in *Guys Like Me*—will see enlisting as the patriotic thing to do, a rational decision. Joining the army right out of high school, Craig recalls thinking, was "The next right step. This is natural, this is normal, this is what you do."[1]

Once in the military, young men are immersed in a hyper-masculine, rigidly hierarchical institution that valorizes violence. Most men veterans have told me that they don't recall working with any women when they were in the service, though they may have crossed paths with a few women who worked in office support or medical jobs. The military "builds men" (again, to draw from an old marine corps slogan), in part by separating men from women, and by disparaging and punishing anything or anybody considered feminine.

But military men's physical and symbolic separation from women does not mean that these men never encountered women. Some of the men veterans I interviewed casually mentioned "getting a woman" or "buying some sex" in Japan, or the Philippines, or Vietnam while on leave from their wars. One recalled how, when his navy ship tied up to a pier for the men to take liberty in a foreign city, "They had a barrel of condoms for you to pick up on your way off the ship." For most men in the U.S. military, women were absent as colleagues, but present either as sex workers or as symbolically disparaged "others" against whom military masculinity is constructed. Anyone who has viewed the depiction of boot camp cruelty in the 1987 film *Full Metal Jacket*, or of the violence of military family life in *The Great Santini* (1979) has glimpsed the ways that misogyny and homophobia are deployed as brutal truncheons to police the perimeters of military masculinity.[2] "The worst thing you could call a marine," I was told by Vic, an 82-year-old marine corps veteran, "was a pussy."

A scholar of gender, war, and peace, Catherine Lutz has written of the military that "there is no workplace more supportive of a masculine identity centered in power, control and violence."[3] That being the case, why would young women enlist? Why, for that matter, would gay, lesbian, queer, or trans people enlist? In this chapter, I introduce six veterans who are part of a younger generation of peace and justice activists: army veteran Wendy Barranco, air force veteran Phoenix Johnson, air force and army veteran Monique Salhab, army veteran Monisha Ríos, marine corps veteran Stephen Funk, and army veteran Brittany Ramos DeBarros. All six are people of color. Three of them are women, one is an Indigenous Two-Spirit person, one identifies as a genderqueer non-binary person, and three others as queer. These six veterans' pathways into the military are similar in some ways to those of the mostly White and mostly heterosexual men I interviewed. Most come from poor or

7.

working-class backgrounds characterized by limited family resources, substandard schools, and racial marginalization.[4] They also frequently grew up surrounded by parents, other relatives, or community members who were veterans. This made military service following high school seem like a rational course of action. Some also saw their military service as an act of patriotism (especially those who enlisted in the aftermath of 9/11). Once in the military, they also confronted some of the same experiences that straight men did, including absorbing the trauma of being in combat zones. But the following six stories also reveal the particularities of service members' experiences—as women, as people of color, as queer—and how these experiences shaped their consciousness and actions as veterans.

Wendy Barranco, U.S. Army, 2003–2006

When people learn that she was deployed in the Iraq War, Wendy Barranco told me, they often gasp and ask, " 'Were you in the front lines?' " She shakes her head in exasperation: "It's like, okay, first of all you know nothing about fucking war. Your ignorance just showed right there." If your boots were on the ground during America's wars in Iraq or Afghanistan, Barranco explained, then you were probably in a war zone with no clear "front lines." Barely out of high school, 19-year-old Specialist Wendy Barranco found herself at the blistering vortex of a war zone—and it was hot in multiple ways. Trained as a combat medic, Barranco spent eight months working in the hospital operating room (OR) in Tikrit, Iraq, from late 2005 to mid-2006, a time of accelerating combat and mounting Iraqi, U.S., and civilian casualties.[5] Barranco found "a sense of purpose and personal fulfillment" in the OR, saving lives of wounded U.S. soldiers and local Iraqis, occasionally while wearing a flack vest to protect against incoming mortar rounds.

At age four, Barranco had moved from her birthplace in Mexico to Los Angeles with her mother. She did well academically in high school, was active in student government and theatre, but her mother's low-wage work in fast food restaurants held little promise as a launch-pad for upward mobility. "I hadn't given much thought to college," she recalls, "I knew that there wasn't any money." But another possible future materialized. Army recruiters "roamed the halls" of her L.A. high school in 2003 as the United States was ramping up its war in Iraq. "I mean, they were everywhere." The teenaged Barranco once had to fight off a drunken sexual advance from her married and considerably older recruiter. Still, she decided to enlist, and part of the reason, she recalls, "was patriotism for September 11, after it happened," and her desire "to give something back to this country that gave my family and I so much." She laughs in retrospect at her youthful naivete: "I was fucking 17. What the fuck did I know about the world? I definitely bought into the propaganda. I bought into the whole defend the country, and terrorists, and blah blah blah. Also, I saw it as an opportunity to travel. I saw it as an opportunity to fund my education. I saw it as an opportunity to go into a field that I always wanted to go in, which was medicine."

Following basic training at "Fort Lost-in-the-woods, Misery, also known as Fort Leonard Wood, Missouri," Barranco received combat medic training at Fort Sam Houston, in San Antonio Texas. In her next stint at Madigan Army Medical Center, near Tacoma, Washington, the dreary weather was "miserable" for a "Southern Cali girl," and the work in the medical clinic was slow and far from challenging. There, she realized, "I'm a nobody. I helped with some minor procedures." But in September of 2005, she received orders that she would deploy to Iraq. "It was scary, but on a certain level, you know it is coming. War time. You're going to have to go at some point." Within a few short weeks, Barranco had been air lifted from Kuwait into Iraq by a C130. "That's I think when, you know, it hit for me. This is happening. This is real. Up until that point there was a sense of this isn't real yet. You don't feel it. It's not tangible. It's not concrete." It got concrete very quickly after she was assigned to the OR in Tikrit.

Almost the first day that I started that position we got a pretty heavy trauma. It was a soldier, and he had gunshot wounds to his chest so when he showed up I mean he had pretty much bled out and we went to the ER to see if he was going to make it to the OR. There was blood fucking everywhere. At that point, you know, his clothes had come off, and looking at that guy on the table, on the bed, was like looking at myself because he was a soldier. He couldn't have been more than 25, and he bled out and he died. At that moment after seeing my supervisor step out, go take a breather, and I saw her cry and just lose it—I was like, yeah. We can't do that. That can't happen. So I decided that I wasn't going to let that stuff get to me. That in order for me to do my job that those feelings were going to have to be put aside. The moment that you let fear or sadness or anything like that, your job becomes compromised. I put it away. Yeah. That guy taught me that lesson. That guy taught me that lesson.

The day-to-day in Tikrit, Barranco recalls, was "like a roller-coaster," a series of frantic highs, "when the shit hits the fan," and relaxed lows, "when you are twiddling your thumbs not doing anything." Overall, she found the work to be deeply fulfilling.

> That time that I spent in the OR was by far some of the best time that I've had just as person, as a person in the medical field. I was good at my job, and I was curious to learn. I was always asking questions. What is this for? I loved it. Like, I grew, I gained so much knowledge, and I was doing what I loved. Yeah, you're fucking covered in blood and guts and whatever the fuck, but like, it is a sense of purpose and personal fulfillment of saving lives. That shit feels good. It does! It really does.

Still, the work was also dangerous and physically taxing.

> There were a couple of times where we're in the middle of surgery and we're hearing incoming mortar rounds. At that point you've got to put your flack vest on but you can't leave. You can't go to hard shelter; you've got to stay with the patient. I didn't really have time to be scared. I mean, there is a couple of times where like I'm drenched in sweat because I have my scrubs [on] and my flack vest and it's not just hot outside but we turn on the heat in the tent to help the patient maintain body temperature. It might be 100 outside or 110, inside it is 150.

The heat in Tikrit was unbearable for Barranco in other ways. She understood the dangers of being in a war zone, but she had not counted on having to fend off continual sexual harassment from the lead doctor in the OR.

> I saw him on the daily. He was a general surgeon. Major. There were times where I'd be running my ass off to the lab to get more blood and I would be alone in those tents and he would fucking appear and just corner me. He would say things like, just, your typical fucking man sexual harassment shit, like, "What are you going to do now Wendy? We're alone. Nobody is around." For the entire fucking nine months, I not only had to do my job, but I had to watch my own back with this guy. That's an added layer of I'm already in a fucking war zone. I'm already having to do my job. Now I have to deal with your ass too, and I can't do anything about it. It's not fun. There's nothing to be done. I mean, the way I saw it was I was dispensable and he

was not. He had rank. He was a general surgeon, an officer and a major. If I had spoken up I was the one who was going to be gotten rid of, not the other way around, no matter if he had raped me or beaten me or anything.

Nor had Barranco expected to have fight off a colleague who attempted to rape her. She awoke from a nap in her sleeping quarters to find the man sitting on the bed watching her sleep. "It got physical. I fucking had to fight him off. I kicked him in the fricking gonads and I scratched him. It was not good. I think he thought that I wanted it, that this was part of the game or the play or whatever the fuck. I'm like, '*No!* Get the fuck *out!*'" A woman sergeant had actually "heard everything that went down" from her nearby quarters.

> She advised me not to say anything. Keep my mouth shut. Keep my head down. Don't cause trouble for yourself. Don't cause trouble for the unit. She's like, "You are close to going home." Around that time I was still waiting to hear if I could go home even, or if I was going to get stop loss. She's like, "You know, if you say something, chances are you're the one who is going to be gotten rid of, so just keep your mouth shut and don't say anything."

This point in her deployment, 2006, was a rough time in the war. Casualties were mounting, and opposition to the war at home was growing. Troop shortages were straining the U.S. effort to sustain the war. As a result, many deployed soldiers were being "stop-lossed"—forced to re-deploy a second time, or even a third or fourth time. Wendy Barranco was certain that she was done with it.

> I was not reenlisting. I did not want to reenlist. At that point I was already questioning my faith. Is there a god? Why would he let this be? Why is there war? Why are people dying? Why is this kid dying? Why are we even fucking here? Finally, it just came one day, they gave me my orders. They are like move the fuck out. You are free to leave country.

As was the case with so many young soldiers returning from this war, Wendy Barranco's re-entry into civilian life was jarring.

> I came back. I landed in Philly in July 4, 2006. At the airport, several people were like, "Oh my god! Let me buy you a drink!" I was like, "not unless you want to get in trouble. I'm not 21." That, for me, I think was an interesting

time in my reflection: I can go off to war, kill motherfuckers, but I can't have a legal drink! That stuff started coming out. All that compartmentalizing stuff started really coming out. I engaged in several not-smart behaviors. Dangerous behavior, because I was seeking that high again. So, I went sky-diving. I did mushrooms. I was speeding. I got pulled over. I got a ticket. All these things to get that chemical rush back. I didn't know what the fuck I was doing.

Barranco enrolled in some classes at Pasadena City College, thinking that she might restart her dream to build a career in medicine. But much of what she experienced in college life just made her angry.

I fucking hated everything and everyone. It just—being around these kids was really triggering. When people would say shit, like the obsession with the latest phone, or the obsession with the latest shoes. Just, oblivious! I felt like I needed to shake them or slap them or something, like "We are in the middle of a fucking war and your greatest concern is the latest Jordans?" Like, "fuck is wrong with you?" I felt used. I felt like a rag that had just been used to clean up a mess and just discarded. By the military. I felt like I was just a rag. You are of no use to us now. Goodbye. You're done here. I strug-gled a lot. Those early years were really shitty.

One day, she saw a sign on the PCC campus, announcing "a forum on vet-erans and their experiences." The program included speakers from a recently formed organization, Iraq Veterans Against the War (IVAW). In retro-spect, Barranco sees her decision to attend as "a life saver" for her. At first, the IVAW speakers' critical commentary on the U.S. war in the Middle East made Barranco "fucking furious." She recalled thinking, "This is bullshit!" She decided to step up to the podium and speak, to tell them what it was re-ally like in the war.

I start talking shit! Literally mid-word towards the end a lightbulb goes on in my head like a fucking cartoon while I'm talking, and I'm like— [pause]—oh, shit! Everything I'm saying—everything I'm saying is exactly what they are saying. And it hit me, and I was like, yeah! I was a fucking pawn, you know? The sexual harassment. The imperialism. All of this! It was like seeing a puzzle for the first time and you put it together and you're like oh, shit: there is the picture. There it is.

Barranco joined IVAW on the spot. "From that day on I got involved." She helped to build a chapter in Los Angeles—mostly with a group of men who were marine corps vets—and before long she was president of the local chapter. Over the next few years, the L.A. chapter of IVAW engaged in a blur of actions, from anti-war forums, to counter-recruitment education, to guerilla street theatre. Barranco had found a group and an organization with whom to heal and engage in action: "It was IVAW that got me on a path of peace, of healing, of questioning, and putting the pieces together in a way that aligns with feminism, with justice, human rights."

Phoenix Johnson, U.S. Air Force, 2003–2007

Still a 17-year-old high schooler, Phoenix Johnson signed up for the United States Air Force's delayed enlistment program. Their[6] 18th birthday cake was emblazoned with *"Happy Birthday Private!"* and three days later, Johnson was off to boot camp. In retrospect, Johnson is amazed that nobody was talking about the fact that the United States was at war. "They invaded Iraq in 2003 and 90 days later I left on a fucking plane to go to boot camp, and nobody said a word. Nobody was like, 'Oh you're about to go to war.'" Eventually, Johnson was disappointed not to be deployed to Iraq during four years in the air force. But Phoenix Johnson's story shows that combat experience is not the only source of military trauma, nor does one have to be a combat veteran to rise to a position of leadership in veterans' peace and justice organizations.

Phoenix Johnson was "in a military environment since birth." Their father "was a career serviceman in the coast guard," and his relationship with their mother eventually came to symbolize, for Phoenix, the ways that militarization, settler colonialism, and racial violence continue to shape the lives of Indigenous people.[7] Born in Seattle, Johnson traces their ancestral homelands to their mother's home, "The Tlingit and Haida territory, just north of Sitka, just north of Bellingham in the west of what we call Canada now." Johnson's father descended from European settlers: "They are the colonizers. They are all White." Sometime in the early 1980s, according to Johnson's rendering, their father came floating in on a cutter and decided this is the woman he wanted to marry. "He grabs her up and drops her off with his family in Oregon, alone away from everything she knows. Hops back on the ship, comes back, they get married, they have me." The marriage did not last.

My father [was] abusive both to her and myself. Well, they split and he strong-armed her in court, and considering all of the children that were being taken from Indigenous families, I was just another product of that. So I grew up with him and engrossed in military culture, taught on a daily basis by an active duty military man who had no parenting or nurturing skills. And there's a racial dynamic too. I was always looked at and treated as the outdoor dog who was just lucky to be inside, and my cousins who were blonde-haired blue-eyed and had both White parents were treated like indoor kittens.

Phoenix "was not a star student," and college "didn't seem like much of an option." Lack of emotional support at home, and demeaning messages about their abilities that they received at school combined to make joining the military seem like the best option.

They were really hard on me, and treating me like I was defective all the time, like "You need the military because you're deformed and you're not American enough and you are probably going to be a whore or a criminal." That was a part of that undercurrent. Not even an undercurrent, a current.

If lack of family and educational support provided a push, military life also provided an attractive pull for the young high school student. "My favorite movie at six was *Top Gun* and there was Tom Cruise, he was so cool with that smirk and those glasses, and I wanted to be just like him! I know it was the navy, but I was like, at six years old, 'I want to work with fighter jets one day.'" Johnson enlisted in the air force at age 17.

Boot camp in the middle of summer at Lackland Air Force Base San Antonio, Texas, "was really hot." Johnson was in "an all-female flight," with a male drill instructor. "We were his first female flight ever. Oh, awful. We were all just garbage. To him we were all garbage." Following some training in air combat command and battle management at Keesler Air Force Base in Biloxi, Mississippi, Johnson was suddenly an 18-year-old woman with "huge responsibilities handed to me."

I'm sitting on mission with 20 aircraft in the air, trying to make sure they don't collide. When we weren't doing that we were doing weapons system evaluation, testing the missiles. I think it was exciting. I felt important. My ego was inflated. That was the pinnacle of my existence as an American citizen, to be an instrument of war and death. I was exactly that. I had the most expensive toys in the air. It was all language of death. I didn't really think about that until a lot later. To know that I had a part in—those guys went and used all those skills that I helped perfect. Those things that came out in the news, like, I helped them do that.

It was exciting work, but in retrospect, Johnson now sees the unhealthy consequences of the constant stress of this "fast-paced environment."

> I think that's where a lot of my anxiety disorder [started]. We were so hyped up—I mean we were screaming on the floor. And then you get off mission and that was it. There's no decompression time there's no talking about what we were doing, so I was just left to go exist ... zone out on my desk, and then on the weekends I would drink way too much like everybody else did. We were put in such a hyper-aware, hyper-adrenaline state all the time—Yeah, "fucking kill the toe-heads! Fucking human garbage!" That's what I heard. Then we'd go off and party hard.

The partying provided neither the emotional decompression Johnson needed, nor the human connection with similar people. "My entire existence on active duty I don't recall having contact with another First Nations person the entire time. There were a couple of other women of color. But I never recognized anybody, I never had anybody who was a friend. Nothing. Nobody."

Many of those Johnson was training were deployed to Iraq. Johnson was disappointed, even felt some "survivor's guilt" for escaping the combat costs for which others were so dearly paying. But Johnson's job took them to Florida, which "was a shit show," and then on to Iceland, where things weren't much better. Florida, Johnson recalls, "was where my terror happened. I was sexually violated in Florida. MST [military sexual trauma] resonates with me. I was drugged once in Florida, by somebody that I worked with." There, Johnson also met and married the airman who later fathered their child. The marriage, Johnson can now see, was a youthful mistake, "a dysfunctional relationship that resulted in domestic violence."

Johnson and their husband were deployed to Luke Air Force Base, near Glendale, Arizona, where Phoenix was trained as an air surveillance technician instructor. The job heaped a stressful burden on top of an already wobbly life. "I was expected to be beyond perfect, which is really hard to do when you are being harassed and abused in your relationship.

That's when my panic attacks started." When Johnson began hyperventilating once on the job, someone accused them of doing it on purpose, "to get attention." Johnson stopped eating, "and was rewarded by being really skinny." Johnson had "tried to get help with the domestic violence case and there was a lot of retaliation because of that and a lot of shitty treatment." When Phoenix then became pregnant, some accused them of faking that as well.

After Johnson had served four years and two weeks in the air force "they dumped me out." Phoenix stayed with their husband for a while, but eventually was "alone, completely isolated, at home in a room." By the time their daughter was born a few months later, Johnson was unmoored.

> I didn't have a baby shower, I didn't have a job. Nothing. It was just her and I. I was going through those painful dysfunctional cycles experiencing symptoms and finding out after the fact that oh, I need treatment for that. I had no idea. I just was left like just a fucking bloody mess for *a while*. So yeah. It was fucking painful, and it was stupid, and I didn't want to be a statistic. I spun out. I spun out hard too. I was angry. I was resentful. I had spent so much fucking time investing in this thing that didn't serve me. Didn't care about me. Was built to destroy me, and at some level I was aware of that but I couldn't articulate it, but I just felt so fucked over by my father, by my commander, by my husband. I had no money, I had no skills to go out in the outside world. My job was not translatable. They say you have a career after the military. You don't have a career after the military. It was demeaning and embarrassing.

Johnson took a $10 an hour job at Walmart, with which they managed, barely, to take care of their daughter. But Johnson felt "no pride, so I got high and I got drunk for like a year straight. I did mushrooms. I did ecstasy. I did ecstasy mixed with heroin and mixed with meth and I got up in the morning and I smoked weed." When a friend told them, "Phoenix, you are an addict," it was "a cold bucket of water." Johnson determined on the spot to stop taking drugs and drinking, and soon thereafter decided to go to school. For five years at Portland State University, with their daughter in daycare and eventually in kindergarten, Johnson studied public health and psychology. They also began to embrace their veteran identity, relishing the opportunity to hang out with other vets at the university's Veterans Center. Johnson came to learn that "we're all a little bit broken. I was getting emotionally invested in what it means to be a veteran. Seeing people struggle so much. Taking my friends' phone calls in the middle of the night."

Johnson took the lead in rejuvenating a dormant veterans' group on campus. "Apparently," they began to realize, "I'm an organizer!" And as Johnson networked, "I started listening to other veterans who had little tidbits to say that were oppositional to the war, and to the system, and I was like, 'that's what I'm thinking!' That's what I was feeling but I didn't know how to say it. I would read things online or talk to people and then I was able to build my own conclusions." Johnson learned about Portland's chapters of Iraq Veterans Against the War and Veterans For Peace, and started hanging out with members.

> People were doing speaking tours and speaking out against the military and going to rallies and speaking in front of crowds of people. I started doing that and I was being asked to speak. We bombed Syria and the local organizers in Portland wanted me to speak on that at the rally. My leadership and organizing skills were worked out and developed. I was helping some folks start a non-profit that specifically served homeless veterans. I was part of the military support network, resources for veterans, creating these events for the veterans at the school. Doing all the things that I now do for anti-war movement stuff. Being politically involved.

Johnson's emergence as a political activist in Portland, from 2013 to 2018, was also a time of tremendous growth in defining and embracing the multiple aspects of their identity.

> I am a Native American veteran. I also identify as a woman, but [also] as a femme-identifying Two-Spirit person.[8] So yeah, we'll use the term "woman of color," because I know that I'm perceived as a non-White person, but I'm also aware I'm on the scale of more—what's the word I'm looking for?—I guess, "White acceptance" because of my light skin. So as a woman of color, I know that that comes with some loose edges.

Too often, the "loose edges" of an intersectional identity like Phoenix Johnson's make navigating daily life a complicated, even perilous challenge. But as we shall see, when grounded in a progressive organizational context, this intersectional knowledge also holds the potential for forging new directions in peace and justice organizing.

Monique Salhab, U.S. Air Force, 1997;
U.S. Army, 1999–2007

During their[9] second Iraq deployment in 2006, Monique Salhab found themselves "being the aggressor, yelling, shoving my rifle in people's faces." When their platoon would storm into an Iraqi village, "You break someone's door down, you're yelling at them and you've got dozens of rifles pointing, yelling. It was chaos." After breaking into a home, the platoon would separate the women and the kids, "who are yelling and crying," to another room or area. Salhab was ordered to "give the women some comfort while their husbands or sons were being interrogated." On one such occasion, a weeping Iraqi mother who "had some broken English" pointed to the name tag printed on Salhab's uniform, and confronted her captor with a penetrating question.

"What are you doing? Why are you doing this? You're one of us!" So after we left out of there, one of the guys was like, "What was that lady saying to you? Why did she keep poking you?" And I said, "Oh, she was just poking at my name." And he was like, "What do you mean?" And I was like, "Well, it's Middle Eastern." He's like, "Wait, you're American, right?" And I'm like, "Yes, I'm American." And he was like, "Well, how'd you end up with that last name?" And I was like, "It's my dad's. You know, my dad's a veteran. He's a naturalized citizen." He's like, "Wait, so what side are you on then?"

Monique Salhab's rendering of this wartime moment encapsulates themes of marginalization that run through their childhood, youth, and decade-long military career. A woman whom some saw as too masculine; black-skinned, but rejected by some African Americans as too "white"; queer, but semi-closeted for much of their life: Where did Salhab fit? What side was Salhab on?

Born in 1975 in Brooklyn to two immigrant parents—their mother was from Panama, their father was Grenadian Lebanese—Monique Salhab spent much of their childhood living in Germany, where their father was stationed. Their "earliest memories are of the military," and Salhab recalls being "fascinated" by the "discipline, the honor, the service" of military life. Salhab's mother was a civilian, but worked "with a lot of other military wives, painting tanks." Their father was "very strict" and "definitely physically abusive." When Salhab was 11, their family moved to hot and humid Fort Campbell,

Kentucky. Their mother was not happy being there. And it was here that young Monique had their "first personal encounter with racism" when an older white girl in the neighborhood put them into a crushing bear-hug, bit them, and admonished Monique, "I don't want niggers playing with my brother."

Soon, they moved back to Brooklyn with their mom, to live with their grandmother. Catholic high school was "the most miserable four years of my life. I didn't fit in. I was an outcast. This popular group of Black kids actually would call me an Uncle Tom, told me that I wasn't Black enough, that I was a Black person acting like a White person." They were also realizing that they were different in other ways. After PE one day, a girl grabbed them and said, "You don't walk like a girl. I'm going to tell everybody that you walk like a man." This did not come as fresh news to Monique—"I knew I was different"—but it was not until their sophomore year in college that they thought, "I can't hide this anymore." When they came out to their mother, it did not go well. "You can't be gay," their mom told them, "You're confused."

Salhab had been admitted to West Point. Their father wanted them to go there, but they decided on Pace University, in New York City. There, they found a group of friends who were queer. With them, "I could breath. I didn't have to lie. I didn't have to pretend." But they did have to mask their queerness in Air Force ROTC. Salhab recalls thinking, "Yeah, this doesn't go well in the military." During their junior year, Salhab resigned from ROTC, concluding, "I just can't do this anymore." Salhab graduated college in 1996, and within a year they were drawn back to the military, enlisting in the Air Force.

Basic training at Lackland Air Force base near San Antonio, Texas, "was a piece of cake," since it was "no worse than what I went through with my dad, you know, whether it's his yelling or beating the crap out of me." But early on, Salhab had moments—such as the time they were holding a hand grenade during training—of "clear awareness" that "I should not be doing this." Stationed in North Dakota, they were often bored, and they "spent a lot of time drinking," which would "drown out" the inner voice that kept telling them, "You know this is wrong. This is not your path." It helped that Salhab connected with a group of five gay women colleagues, and together they struggled to navigate and survive the military's "Don't Ask, Don't Tell" (DADT) policy.

In effect, DADT required people like Monique Salhab and their friends to huddle quietly in the cramped confines of the "camouflage closet."[10] Salhab knew a couple—a man and woman who were both gay—who got married "just to calm the suspicions. He was being harassed by some of the guys in his unit, and then he got married and things calmed down." Salhab managed to have a brief relationship with another woman, but the surveillance of DADT was increasingly oppressive. "I literally felt like my life spirit was being extinguished. Like it was just becoming dimmer and dimmer. I was drinking heavily. I was angry all the time." When Salhab told their superior officer that they wanted to resign, their photograph was posted on "the wall of shame, where they put up pictures up of airmen who were a disgrace to the unit, to the uniform." Eventually, the commander called Salhab in and told them they were going to let Salhab go, but not before deriding them as "a shameful piece of shit."

In 2001, Salhab moved to New Mexico, where they were working for a security company. They had joined the Army Reserve 1998, in part because they still felt they "had to prove myself." When 9/11 happened, they knew they would be activated, and two years later, they were. By then, they had "done a lot of reading" and were decidedly against the war. Salhab had a physical exam at the VA as part of their reactivation, and the doctor was hostile and he raped them. Angry and confused, Salhab decided, "Fuck that. I'm just going to go. I'll go and the likelihood of me being blown up or shot is pretty high, so I won't have to come back and deal with this."

In Iraq, Salhab found themself in a war zone that "was like the wild, wild west, where anything goes. I carried my weapon 24/7. Slept with it, carried it." Following their first stint, they asked to be re-deployed to Iraq, and an officer laughed, "Man, you really want to get yourself some ragheads." Mostly, though, they recall feeling "angry and violated. I wanted to die." Salhab was "abusing pain meds" and "just waiting for someone to shoot me, kill me, get blown up." They suffered no illusions that the United States was doing good for the people of Iraq.

> Going out on a convoy and looking at how much had been just destroyed—everything was just rubble. And I kept thinking, "How are people living? Where are they living?" They're living just on the street next to a pile of rocks. And I was angry at the thought of what we were doing. And I already knew that, but then to see it was like, yeah, these people hate us. They fucking hate us.

There was little reason, either, "to trust any of the men in my unit."

One time, us women were in a separate tent and we all knew we had to be on guard, and two guys snuck into our tent and handcuffed one of the women. There was eight of us in the tent. There was two guys. They had their weapons on us and I knew what they were going to do. And I remember saying, "You don't want to do this." Like, I was bargaining, and I remember saying, "I bet if you just ask us, one of us will be okay with sleeping with you." I don't know why I said that. And one of the guys, he got close enough to one of the girls and she took her rifle and she stabbed him in the stomach with it.

Salhab left Iraq and the military "pretty uneventfully" at the age of 32. Back in Albuquerque, they had "no idea what I wanted to do. I just thought maybe I'd just disappear." Booze, Oxy, Percocet—none of it helped: "the depression just boomerangs so much harder. Definitely wanted to kill myself." Nor did they seek help at the VA: "that's where the doctor raped me."

Salhab mostly "suffered in silence," and for a long stretch was homeless. They worked for a time as an advocate for disability rights in New Mexico, then had a job working in a homeless shelter for men, where they started meeting a lot of veterans. They tapped back in to Buddhism, a spiritual practice Salhab had begun during their ROTC years, and in 2010 they stopped drinking. They met and then moved in with World War II vet Sally-Alice Thompson, a local activist with Veterans For Peace. Previously, while still homeless, Salhab had kept crossing paths with another VFP member, Charles Powell.

I remember one day I said, "Are you following me?" He's like, "No, young lady, Albuquerque is just a small city," and he says, "Are you going to come to a Veterans For Peace meeting?" And I said, "Why do you care?" And then I'll never forget his response. He's like, "Why shouldn't I?" For him it was like, well, why shouldn't I care? I felt like, well, I got to go check this out now. And that's how I ended up at Veterans For Peace.

Thompson and Powell urged Salhab to apply for a scholarship to pay for transportation and lodging at the 2014 VFP national convention. There, in Asheville, North Carolina, Monique Salhab began to immerse themself in VFP. "It was the first time that I had met other 9/11 vets who were just trying to figure their shit out, some who were doing some cool things. And, I was just, 'Oh, wow, this is pretty awesome.' That, for me, was pretty amazing. It really opened up my eyes."

Monisha Ríos, U.S. Army, 1997–1998

When she joined Veterans For Peace in 2015 it didn't take Monisha Ríos long to learn that there is a status hierarchy among vets—even those working for peace and justice. On meeting Ríos, VFP members would ask if she was a combat vet, and Ríos knew immediately that when she said no, "They're not gonna take me seriously, I'm not gonna matter. I won't be considered important. To the work of peace. As a veteran." But it also didn't take her long to settle on her answer that question: "I say, 'I was in *unconventional* combat. As in, every fucking day, I had to fight to not get raped. As a woman in the military. So, yeah. I was in combat.' "

Born in 1970 in St. Petersburg, Florida, Monisha Ríos was raised by her mother, a White woman from New Hampshire, and her Puerto Rican father. After her parents split up, she and her mother lived through "hard times, a lot of stress." Monisha saw her father frequently, and she recalls that he "wanted me to speak English, he wanted me to be American, he wanted me to not go through the things he went through—the discrimination and racism, hatred that he gets, as a—we're Afro-Rican, so some of our features are more African." In school, Monisha "identified as Puerto Rican," and ignorance about Puerto Rico and the ethnic composition of a colonized people, coupled with what Ríos names as "being light-skinned" led to problems. Because of their assumptions about her name, some White people called her a "wigger . . . there was a lot of racism. A lot of people tried kicking my butt."

By the time she was 14 years old, Ríos was seeing military recruiters in her school. Their messages resonated with her, partly because many of her relatives had been in the service, and because she grew up "getting inculcated with war movies and all the glory of it, and you're serving your country, and we're the good guys in the world, and so on and so forth." There were also practical reasons to be drawn to the military. "I was working at McDonalds, and I was like, 'there is no way I am going to afford college working at McDonalds, and I'm not gonna work at McDonalds for the rest of my life,' so, that's what really drove me to the military." Her recruiter gave her an army t-shirt, and she "wore it constantly." While still a junior in high school, Ríos enlisted in the army's delayed entry program. She had a plan: "I was gonna go into the army, retire at 37, come out with that pension, and then go to my home town and then join the police force."

Two weeks after graduating from high school in 1997, she was off to boot camp at Fort Jackson, South Carolina. Placed in one of the first sex-integrated training programs, Ríos found herself "confronted by misogyny" immediately.

> It was blatant. And it was in my face. One of the first things that happened was all the women got taken aside in reception battalion and taught how to not be sluts in the army. So, "Keep your legs closed, don't smile, don't blink your eyes too much, don't batt your eye lashes, don't tilt your head a certain way," like, "Don't be a whore, don't use your femininity to get ahead." Like, basically, "It's on you to not get raped."

The U.S. military in recent years had been rocked by a series of sexual assault scandals, perhaps the most visible being the navy's 1991 Tailhook scandal in Las Vegas, Nevada. In response, the military had instituted some policy reforms, but drill instructors apparently had leeway to interpret policies in their own ways. Ríos recalls that her "Vietnam era" drill sergeant "was just one of those hateful types who went out of his way to pick on the women, to humiliate, in really horrible ways. 4:15 was wake up time—and he came in, yelling and screaming that it smelled like rotting seabass in our barracks." Drill sergeants routinely punish recruits—women or men—with verbal abuse, extra running or push-ups, often for the smallest mistakes or indiscretions. But this DS heaped on extra layers of sexualized humiliation for the women, once punishing Ríos by making her do "flutter kicks" while lying flat on her back, in front of everyone. "I was doing that and then he makes me stop and just have my legs open. Up and open. And then he just starts slinging insults about me being a prostitute and a whore, and my mother was a prostitute and a whore, that's why I came to the military to be a prostitute and a whore, all the men should leave me alone 'cause I am just gonna give them diseases and get them in trouble."

Ríos didn't know what to make of the fact that "this man hated women. He made it a point to say all the time that we were there pussifying his army. That was his favorite thing to say: 'Don't come here and pussify my army.' He hated us being in his military. Hated it." Ríos quickly realized that the army belonged to men, "and we were intruders. We didn't belong here unless we were a nurse, or a prostitute." This same drill sergeant stepped up his abuse of

Ríos when they were in chow hall. "Every time I would bring the fork up to try to eat something, he would make a derogatory comment. Loud enough for everyone to hear. About what body part of a man I was really wanting in my mouth." Ríos sees in retrospect that this is the moment that her eating disorder began.

During her nine-month training at Keesler Air Force Base in Mississippi, Ríos began to suffer from asthma, and the painful shin splints that developed in basic training from the running got worse. Meanwhile her body weight was continually surveilled with BMI caliper tests and "constant body-shaming" that was institutionalized and public: deemed to be too heavy, she was forced into the "Fat Boy Program," which consisted of extra physical training (PT), which in turn exacerbated her shin splints. She found some solace in the friendship she developed with six women in her unit, one of whom confided in her that she could keep her weight down with laxatives, which "soon became a staple."

Sexual harassment continued at Keesler. Seeing her male superior's boots under the shower curtain, just inches from her own feet as she showered alone, terrified her. She covered herself as best she could, but wondered, "What if he tries to rape me? Do I have to let him rape me? I can't defend myself against my superior. What happens if I do defend myself? And that's when my hygiene went to shit, because I was too scared to go to the bathroom. I was too scared to take a shower, unless other women were around."

Once, in a training classroom that was mostly men and perhaps two other women, a male airman she thought was a friend was sitting behind her, bragging about his sexual conquests, about how he enjoyed "rough sex. And like, rape fantasies. And it was gross, and disrespectful, and inappropriate." Ríos turned and told him "to 'Shut the fuck up,' you know, like, 'What is wrong with you,' you know, 'You're being an asshole. Shut up.'" When she faced back forward, he stood and clamped his teeth onto back of her arm, "like a dog on bone—it felt like forever to me that he was just latched on my triceps. And—and it hurt. After he stopped biting me and goes and sits back down, he's like, 'That's how Ríos likes it, likes it rough.'" Ríos, who at the time "was still a virgin," was stunned. Later, after class her assailant warned her not to tell anyone what he had done: "He's like 'I'm gonna kick your ass if you do.'" Ríos didn't tell anyone at first, but when others saw the visible wound on her arm she was sent to the same doctor who had been treating her asthma.

He is the one who told me, "This is just gonna keep happening to you, and it's gonna get worse." He was like, "I've seen so many young women who had been raped, and I don't want that happen to you. We already have enough for medical discharge for you with the asthma. Let's move forward on that and I can get you out." I had a lot of mixed emotions about that. Because I didn't go in the army to get out of the army. I didn't go in the army to fail. I didn't go in the army to—to let some piece of shit stop me. And then, at the same time, I hated it. And I was already depressed. I was already, aside from using laxatives to maintain weight, they had given me a lot of medications— muscle relaxers for the back issue, all kind of stuff for the asthma. I used the muscle relaxers to sleep. I was not eating, I was not sleeping, I was already having acute stress disorder. And major, major depression. I'm barely functioning. And, so that's when I thought, "Okay, I'm gonna get out, and I'll just take the failure." 'Cause that's exactly how I looked at it, as a personal failure.

After ten months and thirteen days in the army, Monisha Ríos, still only 18 years old, was discharged in May of 1998. She recalls feeling "angry . . . sad . . . miserable and just floundering." A first stab a starting school didn't pan out. After some struggles with the VA to access support for the trauma she absorbed during her time in the army, Ríos was told that her problems were caused not by what was done to her in the service, but by her own "adjustment disorder." Ríos now views this as an example of how psychologists deploy a "weaponized diagnosis, to silence dissent. The VA system, it's very similar to military culture in that women are not taken seriously, our needs are not met, things are not designed for us, and it's not safe."

Ríos eventually resumed schooling at the University of South Florida, where she continued to experience rage and brushes with "suicidal ideation." There, she studied psychology from a prominent traumatologist, deepening her understandings of PTSD and committing herself to getting treatment. Her professional training as a clinician was promising, but her personal life was rough. Married in 2011, the relationship ended in 2012. After a time in a homeless shelter, she connected with others who were attempting to re-form the VA system, particularly how it failed to serve women, too often compounding their experiences of military sexual trauma. Ríos had found a cause: "I inserted myself, and started reaching out to people. And asking, 'Did you have this experience? Did you have that experience?' I became somewhat of a leader within the movement. I started a group called Leave No One Behind; it was led by veterans, and informed by MST survivors."

"That was sort of the beginning" of Ríos's political activities. At a craft fair in New Castle, Delaware, Ríos gave a speech in support of MST survivors, and she "called out" the VA hospital for the ways it systematically failed women vets. She gave more speeches at schools, and delivered public comments in 2015 to the U.S. Congress committee on adult sex crimes in the military. Mostly, she recalls, this work "was ignored," but "it was received well by fellow survivors." Through that work, Ríos met Sarah Mess, who encouraged her to join Veterans For Peace. "I joined VFP, not really knowing what I was getting myself into, or what I would learn, or what I would be confronted by, within myself." Around the same time, Ríos found Psychologists for Social Responsibility (PsySR), an organization that in recent years had risen to the challenge of opposing professional psychologists' complicity in the use of torture, which had become normalized during the Bush-Cheney years of escalating war in the Middle East.[11]

> I started seeing more about how psychology is used. As a weapon. For the military. But not just that but it's how we are recruited, it's how we are trained. And how we learn to kill. And enjoy it. And do it on command and think we are doing the right thing. Psychologists make a profit off of all of that. So at the same time, I was also learning more about My Lai, I was learning about Darfur. I was learning about sexual assault *as* warfare, and I was not seeing that talked about in VFP, really.

For the next several years VFP and PsySR became, for Monisha Ríos, the dual organizational loci through which she joined her passions: working with veterans and carving a space in professional psychology from which to work for peace and justice.

Stephen Eagle Funk, U.S. Marine Corps, 2002–2004

As Stephen Funk rolled in to Camp Pendleton, California, for boot camp in the spring of 2002, the U.S. military's "Don't Ask, Don't Tell" policy was still nine years away from its eventual repeal. Funk had known for much of his life that he was gay, and he understood that DADT meant that he'd have to remain closeted in the marine corps. What he perhaps had not expected was to be racially profiled into a job. As the freshly arrived trainees lined up, the officer barked out, "Okay, where's my Asians at?" Funk, who is half Filipino, and a Korean American recruit glanced at each other, raised their hands, and were summarily assigned to the laundry. "Which is a feminine thing to do," Funk told me, "which meant that we are sub human." In short order, the officer continued to segregate people by ethnicity, "like a cartoon version of you: 'Oh, you're a Hispanic, and that means you're going to go in the kitchen.'" Funk's two years in the marine corps is a chronicle of racial, sexual, and gender-based insults and injuries. His story also describes a blossoming, as he emerged from silence to become a powerful voice of resistance against the Iraq war, a stance that landed him in military prison.

Born in 1982 in Seattle, Washington, Stephen Eagle Funk was named after an uncle, Stephen Edward Funk, who had been murdered by drunk fellow soldiers while serving in the military. Stephen's mother, a Filipina, met Stephen's Irish American and Native American father when they were students at the University of Washington. A navy veteran of the American war in Vietnam, Stephen's father was an alcoholic who was sometimes violent. Home life "wasn't a healthy environment," and by the time Stephen was three years old his mother had decided to take him and his two-year-old sister and leave her husband. Others may have thought of Stephen, "He's just quiet," but he can see in retrospect that due to the trauma of family conflict, "I lost my speech. I wasn't able to speak."

Funk knew from an early age that he was gay. His mother, an artist, routinely brought him into circles with "lots of gay friends." He attended "an alternative high school that was very gay-friendly," and his best friend was gay. In school, he "wasn't hiding the fact that my favorite music artist was Madonna. I didn't try to change my voice, and cover up my lisp." Yet, he remained closeted, in part to keep the truth from his grandparents—Catholic immigrants from the Philippines who were helping to raise him—and perhaps also partly because his father had "tried to punish me for being effeminate, for not being into sports." Military service began to make sense to young Stephen.

I didn't want to be gay because that was going to upset my grandma, and I don't want to be gay because my dad's going to hate me. It's just a stupid thing. It would have been so much better if I had just come out in high school and never joined the military. But I think I was supposed to join the military. I was very drawn to the military, partly because I was closeted, had my own kind of questioning about my own masculinity. Basically, not wanting to be gay for other people, but confusing that, and hating on my-self, and punishing myself.

Following high school, Funk enrolled briefly at the University of Southern California, and then in the summer of 2001 he moved to San Francisco with his sister. When the 9/11 attacks happened, he was working two part-time jobs and "wasn't doing anything particularly important to me." Feeling "disillusioned about choices," he just decided, "I don't care. I'm joining the military." He chose the marine corps in part because of his "contentious re-lationship" with his father, a navy veteran. "If you're going to do it," he recalls thinking, "jump in the pool at the deep end. The marines are so hardcore." He also wondered, "Oh, wow. Maybe this will force me out of the closet." Nineteen years old, he tumbled into boot camp, was "herded into cattle lines," sleep-deprived, drill instructors yelling in his face. One lesson he learned early and often:

> Being feminine isn't good for sure. A marine is a masculine thing. A perfect marine would be tall, athletic, masculine, a leader. They would have a high-and-tight, their uniform would be perfectly pressed, and their boots would be perfectly shiny. I think everybody understands that that's how you get ahead in the military is by conforming to that idea. And then even if that's not who you are in real life, you just pretend to be that until that's who you are. It's like a mask, everyone puts on the same mask.

Funk was well aware of how difficult it was for a closeted gay Asian man to convincingly wear the masculinity mask that was so honored in the marine corps. Mostly, he dealt with it by keeping his head down. "It wasn't like I was putting on that mask. I didn't really participate in the misogyny, and all these conversations about women. I didn't pretend, like calling someone a fag or something." His tendency toward silent introversion compounded; as much as possible, Funk passed time alone in his room or in the library. He was not out publicly, but others assumed he was gay, and "there were people who just hated me for being gay." He was proud during weapons training that "I shot the best out of everybody in my platoon." But this small victory was tossed back in his face by a homophobic drill instructor who used him "as a moti-vation" to others: " 'Oh, the fag shot the best! So tomorrow, when we have the final, don't let him shoot the best.' "

The homophobic humiliations accumulated like constant gut-punches. On one occasion the drill instructor gathered the men in lines, drilling them to perfect their parade rest postures. "They're trying to emphasize the look of the hands in the back, which is, you've got to have your hands in this diamond shape in the back. He said, 'Pretend that you're covering your butthole, and that Funk is standing right behind you.' And I'm in a platoon of people, and I can't say anything, and I'm just an open joke to everybody." Under the suffocating Don't Ask, Don't Tell policy, Funk or other queer service people knew that they risked getting discharged—or worse—if they disclosed their gay identity. While Funk's enforced silence left him with a dull blade, his DI wielded the razor edge of homophobic insult at will, using it to divide, shape, and control his charges. Funk came to understand that his personal humiliations didn't simply marginalize him, but also kept others in line, including "straight people who were like, 'I got to hide being feminine at all,' you know? And there's people who are skinny and short and fat, and they don't fit that kind of ideal of masculinity. You're punished to the degree of how off of that ideal you are."

The "racism and sexism" and "all the microaggressions" were wearing him down. By 2003 he had moved to reserve status, was living in San Francisco again, and going to monthly weekend marine drills in San Jose (Figure 2.1). In S.F., he started attending the growing demonstrations against the war in Afghanistan, and in opposition to the imminent U.S. invasion of Iraq. Bouncing between anti-war activities in S.F. and his reserve weekends in San Jose was feeling increasingly incongruous: "Having the marine haircut at a rally is a bit stark." He tried once or twice to talk with his fellow "weekend warriors" about his anti-war sentiments, but the conversations went nowhere: "They'd say, 'What are you doing talking about this?' And they'd tell somebody in charge of us, and then I had to do push-ups."

Funk began to explore leaving the marine corps as a conscientious objector. He knew he could get discharged simply by coming out as gay, but that didn't feel right. "Certainly, I'm gay, and it sucks to be gay in the military, but my biggest problem with being here is that I don't like being forced to be a violent person. I don't want to participate in an illegal war." Eventually an officer called Funk on the carpet for his anti-war activities, but by then Funk had spoken with a lawyer and assembled a conscientious objector claim. He knew the claim would take some time, but when his reserve unit was activated to go to war, "all of a sudden, I was in hyper drive."

Figure 2.1 U.S. Marine Corps Lance Corporal Stephen Funk, 2003
Photo by Jeff Paterson, courtesy of Stephen Funk

The war in Iraq was ramping up fast, and Funk was clear he did not want
to go. "I didn't want to shine my shoes, get the haircut. I didn't want to salute
officers. I didn't want to pretend anymore, and I needed a way out. It was so
much easier to just say, 'I'm gay.' But instead, I did the hard thing, and then
on top of it, I did it publicly, which was inviting trouble. I was the first who
was punished—because I went public—no other conscientious objector was
punished." Funk had failed to show up for one of his weekend training sessions in San Jose, and the marine corps announced they would court-martial
him for desertion. "There was no map for me," he recalls, but he found allies,
some of them conscientious objectors from the Gulf War who had reached
out to him. Together, they developed a support network, and helped to start
"Courage to Resist," an organization that still exists today to support "military
war resisters who refuse to fight."[12] Going public, for Funk, "was a catalyst for

me to finally talk. I learned how to meet people. I learned so much that I had been deprived of. I was giving keynote speeches at conferences. I was flying everywhere." He also seized this as the opportune moment to publicly come out as gay. "It was exhilarating."

For having missed one weekend of duty, Stephen Funk was court-martialed and convicted. At age 21, he was sentenced and served five months in military prison at Camp Lejeune, in North Carolina. Conservative radio personality Rush Limbaugh lambasted Funk on his radio show. Funk recalls that Limbaugh contrasted him with the heroic (and, as it turned out, largely fabricated) war story of Jessica Lynch. Funk paraphrases his memory of Limbaugh's radio message: "Now, here's this hero, PFC Lynch who is a woman, and she's more heroic than this fag." Funk found his time in prison to be "somewhat liberating." There, he was regularly visited by local Quakers, who have a long history of conscientious objection to war. "They were so full of light and they were a very centered and calming presence to come and visit me every week." When he left prison, his Quaker friends provided him with fresh clothes and transportation.

Released from prison in 2004, Funk returned to San Francisco and stepped up his anti-war work. He was impressed with Veterans For Peace members' "face-to-face groundwork organizing," and the way they were consistently visible at public events, waving VFP banners. At the 2004 VFP convention, a group formed IVAW. Funk was invited to join, and at an anti-war march in Fayettesville, North Carolina, he met other IVAW members for the first time. It was a time of "explosive growth" in the peace movement and in IVAW. For the next decade and more, Stephen Funk dove in: "There was this great momentum. It was a free-for-all. It was kind of crazy, and great, and amazing."

Brittany Ramos DeBarros, U.S. Army, 2012–2018

When she stepped to the microphone wearing her About Face t-shirt to deliver her speech at the Poor People's Campaign "Call for Moral Revival" in Washington, D.C., Brittany Ramos DeBarros recalls feeling "very emotional. My whole body was shaking uncontrollably." The June 2018 speech launched DeBarros into national visibility as a leader among the next generation of anti-war veterans. And her opening words were a powerful statement of where her feet were planted:

My name is Brittany Ramos DeBarros. I am a woman. I am White, I'm
Latina, I'm Black, I'm queer, and I'm a combat veteran. As a person existing
at the intersection of these identities, I carry a grave conviction in my core
that there can be no true economic, racial, or gender liberation without
addressing the militarism that is strangling the morality and empathy out
of our society.[13]

This was more than a public coming-out statement for DeBarros, though
it was certainly that. And it was also more than a smart articulation of
the need to draw together the race, class, and gender struggles for social
justice. It was also a throwing-down of the gauntlet against militarism
and war, at a moment when DeBarros was still serving as a captain in
the U.S. Army Reserve. In the back of her mind was the two weeks of
training duty facing her in just a few weeks. But at that moment, she realized she had done something irreversible. "A line was drawn in the sand.
I felt accountable. I had made a commitment publicly that I will not support this."

Born in Phoenix, Arizona, in February 1989, both of Brittany's parents
were in the army. She describes her mom as "a White woman with blue eyes
from Indiana," and her father, "a Black Puerto Rican man" who "had really warped interpretations about race." Common to many raised in colonized Caribbean cultures "where to be Black is seen as the lowest of the low,"
Brittany's dad "was deeply and explicitly anti-Black . . . and he saw me and my
White-passing abilities as a success of his." Many of Brittany's earliest family
memories "are of violence." She felt betrayed when she was nine years old and
her father suddenly moved back to Puerto Rico, and she learned years later
that his abrupt departure was because "he had warrants out for his arrest, that
my mom had filed about his abusiveness."

Her father hated being in the army, she learned later, and had only joined
because he had been given a choice to enlist or go to prison. Her mother,
however, was an officer, and this became a source of prideful "girl power"
for young Brittany. "You know how little kids on the schoolyard will be like,
'Oh, my dad could beat your dad up.' Then I would be like, 'Oh, yeah? Well,
my mom's in the army.'" After she moved with her mom to Texas, Brittany
attended "really good schools in a hyper-competitive environment." In
middle school, she got involved in a Pentecostal mega-church, and "I threw
my whole self into it. I got super into my youth group and religion, and became very, very dogmatic." She was competitive, "evangelizing in the mall"

with her youth group on Friday nights, striving to rack up the largest number of people who would agree to pray with her.

In high school DeBarros joined the debate team. Learning to research social issues and argue either side helped her in "building the critical muscle" that would so benefit her later. In debates about the U.S. wars in Iraq and Afghanistan, DeBarros could argue either side, but eventually "became known" for her arguments for equality and justice within the military. Denying gays or lesbians the right to serve, or preventing women soldiers from serving in combat, she had come to believe, "is bullshit." She had not yet developed a critique of "the harms of war," and she believed that "even if military policy was harmful in certain instances, that we were this force for good in the world." The problems faced by women, and by gays and lesbians in the military, she believed, resulted from poor leadership. She'd have to enlist, she reasoned, work her way up the ranks, and provide more enlightened leadership.

DeBarros won an ROTC scholarship at the University of Miami, and at first she was a star cadet. But sophomore year she descended into a deep depression, "18 years' worth of trauma" suddenly surfacing. It probably didn't help that despite the fact that she was "obviously attracted to women, I was not out as queer. I wasn't conscious that I was denying it. It just didn't even occur to me. It was so far outside the scope of what I thought was possible, or had been instilled in me in the church." Her depression may also have been fed by her new ROTC drill instructor, "a huge asshole." She recalls his verbal abuse: "Fat shaming, body shaming. He was walking alongside me during a march, I was fit and keeping up, yet he was just screaming at me, like, 'Pick it up, DeBarros, you're a piece of shit.' Then he was like, 'Your ass looks like you swallowed a goddamn Volkswagen Beetle.' "

DeBarros managed to complete college and received her officer's commission. She asked to be trained in ordnance—a "dangerous" specialty with "masculine credibility"—but instead she was trained as a quartermaster, in supply management. She knew that her rank would not automatically bring respect to her as a leader. She'd have to work for that.

There is a classic trope in military war films. A new junior officer, fresh out of college, is greeted by older, hardened, war-seasoned charges who are skeptical about their green new commander. In the movies, this fresh-faced college graduate is always a man, and usually tall and White. In this case, freshly arrived Second Lieutenant Brittany Ramos DeBarros was a woman, brown-skinned and short in stature. "I was the youngest person in the platoon, and

I was the least experienced person in the platoon, as a boss." The men she was in charge of in her platoon "saw me as this straight out of college coed. I was cute, right? I was fit. I was very, very much objectified when I came into that unit. I remember having superiors of mine laughing and telling me like, 'Oh, I was in the motor pool and I heard the soldiers talking about your ass,' and laughing about it, and telling me the story like it was hilarious."

At Fort Bliss, Texas, DeBarros arrived for a month of pre-mobilization preparation as maintenance platoon leader, in charge of forty men. She knew that within a month her platoon would be deployed to Afghanistan. DeBarros worked hard to build rapport with the men serving under her command, treating them with respect, "like experts in their jobs." She pretended not to see the "naked women posters hanging up in the motor pool," and managed to "win the respect of the platoon" when she "bought a 'Firefighters of Miami' calendar and I hung it up under one of the posters, and I was like, 'Equality.' That broke the ice a little bit. People laughed."

Despite her efforts, she never could "break the ice" with the platoon sergeant she was paired with, a man who "was known for having an anger problem and just barking and screaming at people all the time." DeBarros tried to communicate, to build a team with the sergeant, but "there was no budging. He would not communicate with me." Things came to a head when he began "screaming at me in the motor pool in Afghanistan." As his superior officer, DeBarros told him to stop, and asked him to come into her office to talk. There, things escalated. After some back-and-forth, "He said, 'You're not the boss of me.' I told him, 'I'm an officer in the United States military, so actually, I am your boss, so you have to listen to me.' He began screaming and threatening me until I screamed back, 'Get the fuck out of my office.' 'Oh, you wanted me in your office. Now I'm here and you're telling me to get out.' So I stormed towards the door to leave instead. He held the door shut and physically pinned me against my own office wall, looming over me with his hand cocked back like he's going to punch me."

DeBarros reported this incident to her commander, "a cover-your-ass kind of guy," who the next day fired DeBarros from her platoon leader job and relegated her to working as a "strategic communications officer," a newly invented position of which the battalion commander told DeBarros, "brigade said we have to have it, I don't give a shit if you do nothing."

I was so devastated. That was one of the most crystallizing moments: I'm in this combat, this war zone, right? With these people who are supposed to be on my team and they've watched me for months bend over backwards trying to figure out how to work with this guy. They know that this guy is abusive to soldiers, right? Then, when push came to shove, decided to punish me. It's so clear how disposable I was to them.

The Obama administration had announced that the United States was drawing down its mission in Afghanistan and would leave in two years, by 2014. DeBarros's job was to help with this transition, serving as liaison with Afghani civilians and police. She was good at it, and it opened her eyes to "my own humanity and their humanity."

I had a gift for building rapport with people across culture. And I think because I was a woman, it was disarming. I'm spending all this time with Afghan people. And I could not *not* see their humanity. Now, when I'd hear these racist conversations with U.S. and the NATO troops, and they're talking about these places as a shit hole, and these people are barbarians and I hope the whole place just fucking blows up, I'm thinking of a family I had dinner with and of all of these people.

By the time she returned stateside in March of 2013, First Lieutenant DeBarros was convinced "we were doing more harm than good" to the Afghan people. Back in New York and in the reserves, she "really struggled. I was going through these motions, kind of paralyzed. I knew that I wanted to be done with military and felt trapped by my contract." She didn't want to think of herself as a "victim," was "super determined not to have PTSD," and only reluctantly went to the VA to get some help. She "took some time to think" and educate herself about "a bigger picture, about the truth of the context of the war." While working for a non-profit, DeBarros "started to process my deployment, and people's lack of awareness about the wars, and I was venting a lot to my friends about how it was so erased, it was so quiet, that no one even knows the wars are still going on." She wrote two short pieces that appeared on Veterans Day, in 2014 and 2015 on the Living Cities blog. The first, "Four Things You May Not Know About Veterans," was "a bit dry," expressing "kind of centrist, politically neutral position." A year later, DeBarros's political analysis had sharpened, and her piece, "One Female Veteran's Experience," was "more emotional, more charged."[14]

DeBarros started speaking more about the war, and was taken aback to meet many "social justice people who are very educated [on] racial justice and economic justice and just have no idea about the military, you know? I think that probably started planting a seed for me that there was more work for me to do." The public debates when NFL Football player Colin Kaepernick "took a knee" during the national anthem to protest racist violence against Black people was "an ah-ha moment" for her about how "support the troops" rhetoric was being used as a bludgeon to silence dissent against racism. She wrote a long Facebook post "about how what Colin was doing was patriotic," and she started to think that perhaps she had a role to fill in social justice circles. "I should be using my position as a veteran to speak to this specifically . . . I wasn't even thinking I should start speaking out against the war. I was like, I have to start addressing this, these things, for racial justice. That was the entry point for me."

DeBarros "started attending protests for 'Black Lives Matter,'" and she imagined creating a veterans' social justice organization. Searching online to see if any such groups already existed, she found Veterans For Peace. DeBarros decided to attend a local VFP chapter meeting, which turned out to be mostly older men of the Vietnam War era. Luckily, she recalls, Matt Howard, a younger About Face member, was there to speak about the Post 9/11 veterans' group.

I was just like, Oh my God. I was trying not to overreact with excitement because I didn't want to make other people feel badly, because I was really excited about this other group as opposed to VFP, but my eyes were probably widening as he was talking. I was just like, these might be the people I'm looking for, you know? That was 2017. I was super ready to get involved, ready to go.

DeBarros also joined the Poor People's Campaign in 2017, and as her activities and speeches became more publicly critical of militarism and war, she drew the ire of her commander. When she began posting one fact a day about the wars to her Twitter while on training orders, the army began a formal investigation of her. Her superiors were irritated by DeBarros's escalating public actions with About Face in 2018—including a Veterans Day protest in Philadelphia, when Joe Biden presented George W. Bush with the Liberty Medal, and getting arrested while protesting the mistreatment of migrants at the U.S.-Mexico border. The army's investigation recommended "to court-martial me for conduct unbecoming an officer when it became clear I hadn't technically violated any regulations." Perhaps suspecting that DeBarros might use a court-martial as a platform from which to raise public awareness about war, the army took another tack. Knowing DeBarros had an injured foot that required surgery, they offered her an early discharge to the Inactive Ready Reserves (IRR). She filled out the necessary papers and waited. The process "stayed in limbo" for several months, extending beyond the end of her contractual service requirement. Finally, DeBarros told her commander that since the discharge orders had yet to come, she intended to hold a press conference and resign her commission. Immediately, almost like magic, she was granted her discharge the next day. "I won't lie. I was quite tickled by forcing their hand on that."

***

Initially, the six stories in this chapter may read like solo trajectories. But it doesn't take much imagination to see how these six individuals' experiences differ in substance and in degree from those of most straight, White men in the service: absorbing gender hostility and sexualized body shaming from drill sergeants during basic training; enduring sexual harassment or homophobic taunts from superior officers; being disrespected as a leader because of your sex; surviving sexual assaults from other soldiers and domestic violence from partners.[15] When these individuals eventually became active with veterans' peace organizations, their shared experiences of military sexual trauma, coupled with race, class, gender, and sexual marginalization, shaped a situated knowledge that drove their collective understandings, strategies, and actions in their work for peace and justice.

Writing in response to American society's tendency to celebrate famous leaders such as Martin Luther King, Jr., César Chávez, or Rosa Parks as heroic drivers of historic change, Angela L. Davis has written, "It is essential to resist the depiction of history as the work of heroic individuals in order for people today to recognize their potential agency as a part of an ever-expanding community of struggle."[16] This book zeroes in on the experiences and stories of six everyday individuals, many of whose actions are certainly worthy of admiration. But it is their collective work in movement organizations, not their individual heroics, through which they intend to make history.

Interlude 2
Guys being guys

Now checked in to the hotel for the 2019 Veterans For Peace national convention in Spokane, I roll my suitcase to the elevator doors so I can head up to my room. To my right, I notice a half-dozen young Asian women, smartly dressed in identical flight attendant uniforms, standing with their roller-bags. They too are checking in to the hotel, following what I presume was a long work day. The elevator door to my left slides open, and I enter with three White guys, each decked out in VFP t-shirts and hats. They are older—my guess is mid-70s—and a couple of them are heavy-set and laboring a bit as they sidle into the elevator. One leans heavily on a cane. These three guys seem like old friends, happy to see each other and engaging in friendly banter. As the elevator doors close and the four of us start to rise, one of the guys says, "Hey, maybe we should go back down and invite those stewardesses to join us in our room?" The guy with the cane guffaws, and replies, "As though!"—a self-mocking reference, I assume, to the fact that these guys are really old. There is more chuckling and shuffling of feet as the doors open for my floor.

As I exit the elevator, I wonder how long it has been since flight attendants were called "stewardesses." And it strikes me that this kind of casual joking among men, in the absence of women, is very familiar to me, as someone who has studied men's sport culture.[1] Banter about sex, I know, forges erotic bonds among men, and when women are the targets of sexual joking, this affirms the heterosexuality of this connection. Even with these older men, the joke about picking up the "stewardesses," and the self-deprecating retort about their own ageing bodies, apparently succeeds in cementing this sort of male bond.

The men's elevator banter is not only familiar to me, it also strikes me as pretty harmless. But as the three-day VFP convention progresses, and I witness a cohort of younger women of color veterans confronting the older male leadership for their sexism and for their "White savior" modes of working in political coalitions, the meaning of that moment in the elevator thickens. It reminds me of how some of the men veterans I spoke with while doing research for *Guys Like Me* had casually mentioned "getting a woman" or "buying some sex" in Japan, or the Philippines, or Vietnam while on leave from their wars. I wonder if the three men's elevator banter conjured memories—perhaps a half-century or more in the past—of such times for them. And as I get deeper into listening to the stories of the women of color vets, I become more and more aware of how, even among VFP men with decades-long creds as radical activists, their casual sexism, perhaps connected with the racial and colonial privileges of having been members of occupying armies, was too often still largely unexamined, and was perhaps still manifesting in their peace activism.

See Monique's role as an "occupier" on p 30 — not a lot different!!

3

"Rip off the band-aid"

A new generation confronts the veterans' peace movement

A member of the VFP Board of Directors had told me to expect "fireworks" at the business meeting later that morning, and he wasn't kidding. I sat rapt with about 300 VFP members as, for roughly two hours, a group of mostly women of color criticized the board and the organization, encouraged the membership to engage in critical self-examination and dialogue, and implored it to change its business-as-usual practices, especially those that continued to alienate and marginalize women and people of color members.

The most electric moment was when Monisha Ríos joined the meeting remotely, her face appearing on a screen so large I could not help but think of a massive Jumbotron towering over viewers in a stadium. In a thoughtful, precise, and emotionally charged presentation, the army veteran and former VFP board member excoriated the leadership of the organization for what she saw as their shielding of a longtime male leader from numerous accusations of sexist bullying of women members in the organization. Ríos was participating remotely for a reason. A month earlier, she had told me in an interview that she would not be attending this 2019 convention in Spokane, because at the 2018 VFP meetings she had been "sexually harassed and groped." The VFP gatherings, she said, "needed to be made safe" for women, people of color, and queer people. Ríos had also recently left her position as a member of the board. She'd been recruited to join the board a couple of years ago, she said, and then found that her words were most often ignored. Even worse, an older White man on the board routinely interrupted her and talked over her. After she had raised her voice and expressed her frustration, she said, she learned that another board member was labelling her as "unstable" behind her back.

As the VFP board members sat quietly behind a long table on a raised stage, facing the mostly seated membership, speaker after speaker came to the front of the room, often echoing and supporting Monisha Ríos's words. Brittany

Unconventional Combat. Michael A. Messner, Oxford University Press. © Oxford University Press 2021.
DOI: 10.1093/oso/9780197573631.003.0003

DeBarros—a year after delivering her rousing speech in Washington, D.C., and just months after escaping a near court-martial and receiving her discharge from the army—stepped forward. She had not expected to speak, she told me later; after all, she was more active in About Face, and only peripherally involved in VFP. But during the run-up to the convention she "had been hearing from Monique and Monisha, about how frustrated they were," and by the time the group gathered in Spokane, "we all from that moment became like a tight-knit little posse." When she heard Ríos and Salhab speak, DeBarros felt moved by the moment. DeBarros's speech was at once precise, measured and passionate. Perhaps drawing on her experience of having been disrespected as an Army officer, DeBarros put an exclamation point on Monisha Ríos's point about the gendered racism of double standards. White male leaders who raise their voices in meetings are viewed as "passionate," DeBarros observed, "The moment I have rage, I'm 'unstable.'"

An older White woman rose to speak, urging calm, and imploring the membership to have patience with VFP's efforts as "a work in progress." An African American woman veteran objected: "It's not a 'work in progress': Time's up!" and her comment met with an immediate cheer of support from a segment of the audience. This exchange, I think, was deeply resonant of the different knowledge standpoints of the VFP old guard and the more diverse cohort of newcomers. A slogan like "Time's up!" might seem at first like a simplistic dismissal of decades of work done by longtime movement activists. But the slogan resonates with younger members precisely because it echoes the critical analysis emanating from racial justice movements like Black Lives Matter, with which some of these younger vets are affiliated. "Time's up!" encapsulates decades, some might say centuries, of people of color's impatience with White liberals' calls for patient, gradualist approaches to progressive social change. In her book *Unapologetic*, writer and community organizer Charlene Carruthers captured this sentiment: "When liberals say we need change in moderation, I hear 'not you' and 'not yet.'"[1]

Monique Salhab added their own powerful statement at the Spokane meeting. Like Monisha Ríos, Salhab explained that they recently had been an elected member of the board and had experienced disrespect. Salhab implored the membership not to get defensive, not to feel that they are being "called out" as being bad people. Instead, Salhab said, "We are calling you in" to a critical dialogue that is necessary for the good of the organization. Though it may be painful, this discussion cannot wait, Salhab emphasized. It's time for VFP to "rip off the band-aid."

As I listened to Ríos, Salhab, DeBarros, Phoenix Johnson, and others who spoke at the VFP convention, I could not help but see a parallel between them and another group of political activists: "The Squad," four women of color who in 2018 had ridden into the U.S. Congress on a wave of progressive grassroots organizing. After arriving in Washington, D.C., Congresswomen Alexandria Ocasio-Cortez (New York), Ilhan Omar (Minnesota), Ayanna Pressley (Massachusetts), and Rashida Tlaib (Michigan) wasted no time in throwing down the gauntlet, not just with the U.S. Congress, but also with the timid gradualism of their own Democratic Party. The constituents in The Squad's diverse communities were impatient for change. Time was up on business-as-usual, they asserted, as they pressed for a Green New Deal, national healthcare, racial justice, and an end to Islamophobia. I gingerly suggested this parallel to some of the VFP women whom I later interviewed. Monique Salhab chuckled when I mentioned this. Monisha Ríos laughed too, adding, "Yeah, you're not the only one to make that comparison." The group's intervention at the VFP board meeting hadn't just spontaneously happened, Ríos told me. Several of them had been planning this moment together. "It's really beautiful the way it all came together. It started with Mo [Salhab] and I, and grew into this. And we are gonna keep going, we got more plans. So, like, Congress has their Squad; VFP has their Squad too!"

Over the next day I listened intently as VFP members processed this moment of creative disruption. I spoke informally with several VFP members and listened to reactions from the older White men that ranged from defensive dismissal to sincere critical engagement. Two White men, longtime VFP members, expressed dismay with the amount of time that had been spent discussing women of color members' complaints, fearing the discussion would serve as a "distraction" from the central work of the organization. "VFP needs to stay focused on our mission," one of them told me, "to promote peace in the world." Other men, though, were more circumspect, more open to critical dialogue. Joe, an 83-year-old White VFP member, seemed to see the "calling-in" as a bit of a revelation, and a welcome challenge: "I guess we old guys in VFP are just so stuck in our old patriarchal ways of thinking . . . but I'm not so sure where we go from here." Steven, a White VFP member in his 60s, expressed a critical, self-reflexive view: "You know, the older members of VFP are longtime progressives, so even if we have not experienced the same things that these women have experienced, when they criticize us for sexism, or for racism, I'd like to think that we are able to listen with some self-awareness, and then change our behaviors. We have to."

Santiago, a Latino VFP member expressed this sense of urgency even more bluntly: "The VFP good old boy's network is going away. It has to."

Most of the older VFP men I spoke with were neither dismissive nor fully embracing of the challenges laid down by the new generation of veterans, instead expressing mixed, perhaps somewhat muddled, views. A prime example is Michael, a White Vietnam-era veteran in his late 70s, who has contributed decades of service to progressive movements, including especially to VFP. When I asked him to comment on how VFP should respond to the younger members' challenges in Spokane, he replied, "The Black women, they are very radical. And it makes sense; they have been through a lot. But my feeling is that if they want to make change in VFP, they gotta join, put in the time, and make their points about what we should be doing." On the one hand, Michael's statement acknowledges how gendered racism (of the sort I illustrated in Chapter 2) created especially heavy burdens for women of color veterans: "they have been through a lot." On the other hand, his comment seems to assume that VFP is a gender-neutral and race-neutral organization, that all any individual needs to do is to "join, put in the time, and make their points about what we should be doing." The central goal of this chapter is to illustrate how VFP and About Face, like all organizations, are structured by gender, race, and sexual inequalities that create systemic obstacles for women, people of color, and LGBTQ2S "others," to full participation as members and as leaders.[2]

The VFP Squad and their allies value VFP and admire the decades of work the older members have done for peace. But they also share an impatience with the rate of change in the organization. Several weeks after the Spokane convention I interviewed Monique Salhab. I was intrigued by their comment to the VFP membership, imploring them to "Rip off the band-aid," I told Salhab, and I asked, "What do you imagine is underneath the band-aid?"

> It's pus. It's this oozy pus. I feel still very young into this organization, six years. But I don't know how many times I've heard about how women have been treated in the organization, or how women are dismissed in the organization, or how there's no queer or trans presence in the organization . . . The organization has not been able to deal with its internal levels of racism, homophobia, and misogyny. The band-aid is just trying to keep it covered and not get it more infected. No, rip it off, just let it come out.

This small group of younger women and nonbinary people of color and their allies had now thrust the troubling problems of race, gender, and sexual marginalization within VFP into the foreground of discussion. The sense of urgency was palpable, and the future of the organization seemed to hang in the balance. A week after the meetings, I interviewed a board member considered by members of The Squad to be an ally. He said, "These younger members, they won't take this crap any more. Especially the younger LGBTQ vets are watching closely to see what we do. They are the future of VFP," he asserted, "and if the board doesn't do something about it, they may just leave VFP."

The story of the Spokane intervention introduces the themes and purpose of this chapter, to build a critical examination of the internal workings of VFP, and to a lesser extent About Face. I draw from interviews and observations to illuminate the routine mechanisms that marginalize women of color and LGBTQ2S veterans. In what follows, I highlight how gendered racism affects the ways that people think about what a leader should look like; how race and gender tokenism operate; how everyday informal processes like microaggressions and gaslighting alienate and marginalize women, people of color, and LGBTQ2S people; how gendered double-standards operate with respect to expressions of emotion in social movement organizations; and how some longtime members' singular focus on "the mission" of the organizations clashes with the more expansive views of newer members. Along the way, I also point to this new, diverse cohort's strategies for organizational change.

The art of tokenism

To persist over time, any social movement organization has to recruit new and younger members. And any self-respecting progressive organization today will try to recruit in a way that diversifies its membership. But VFP has long been an organization dominated by men, and despite its efforts in recent years, its aging membership remains modally White men veterans of the Vietnam era. Joe, a VFP member in his 80s, laments that VFP remains "mostly men," and his chapter's attempt to recruit younger vets "hasn't been very successful. When they walk in and see all this gray hair, it's a turnoff, I'm sure. And that's a problem." Santiago agrees: VFP, he said, is "very much an older male organization still, and trying to attract the younger generation.

But if anything, the younger generation would probably be more attracted to About Face right now. Because VFP, it's pretty homogenous. There's not a lot of people of color personally that I've met."

About Face does have a younger, more racially diverse membership, and women—including Brittany DeBarros—currently hold key positions of national leadership. This has not always been the case. In the years following the 2004 formation of About Face (then called Iraq Veterans Against the War), Stephen Funk recalls,

> IVAW, it was very wild, wild west, and there was a lot of people who weren't really mature, who were sexist and misogynistic and homophobic. There were all sorts of problems and too much testosterone. We would have these overwhelming majority of people that were bros at a convention, and that just made it monolithic. It was a turn-off to a lot of female veterans [and] in a way I did already feel separated for being queer. I think a lot of people, especially near the beginning, wouldn't want to join just because of the atmosphere was a bit too boys' club.

Over time, Funk explained, About Face opened up, to the point where now "there is a lot more female leadership; everything is more woke." Funk attributed this opening up partly to some of the less serious "bros" having left the organization, and others simply maturing over time. He also points to a "natural alliance" that developed among gay men and women in About Face, people who in the military and in the early years of IVAW had common experiences of marginalization from the ways that "misogyny overlaps with homophobia."

Several of the veterans I spoke with drew a stark contrast between the two organizations, viewing VFP as an older White male organization moving glacially, at best, toward recruiting a younger and more diverse cohort, and About Face as the younger more "woke" organization that had been "doing the hard work" needed to grapple with its internal sexism and homophobia. Brittany DeBarros certainly views the two organizations this way. One of her first experiences in About Face was when she was invited to organize a workshop on patriarchy that was linked to another workshop on White supremacy. She was deeply impressed with About Face's "sense of community" and leaders' commitment to "proactively educate your membership about the connections between White supremacy, patriarchy and militarism." But when she entered VFP spaces, she said, she was disappointed with "the lack of basic wholeness" with which people discussed these sorts of connections. Or even worse, when VFP members dismissed the topics, implying ". . . We already talked about racism, so we're good. We know racism is a thing. What else do you want from us?"

The first time I interviewed Phoenix Johnson, and suggested this sort of VFP vs. About Face contrast, Johnson winced and said, "I wouldn't be so quick to assume that." Johnson had done some work with About Face and had been surprised to be "tokenized" by About Face leadership as one of two Indigenous women in the organization. "I know that they've tried to outwardly look like they're diversifying and they started this decolonizing thing [but] I hate the way they treated me." During Johnson's brief time in an About Face chapter, a "White feminist woman" in the group labelled them "Pocahantas," and accused them of trying to "entrap this White guy by getting pregnant by him or something. And we weren't dating, we weren't sleeping together. It wasn't romantic. But for her to be so sexually degrading and racist like that was really gross." Johnson left About Face, and after moving to the Seattle area, joined a welcoming VFP chapter that opened space for them to rise to a position of leadership (Figure 3.1).

Most veterans I spoke with will draw a distinction between VFP and About Face that presents the former as older, stodgier, male, and White, and the latter as more diverse and "woke," but as Phoenix Johnson's experience illustrates, this distinction is not absolute. Even About Face, as one veteran summed it up, "still has plenty of internal work to do" before it is fully inclusive.

A key dynamic that prevents an organization from moving from a commitment to diversity, to truly embracing inclusiveness is the extent to which new members who were recruited to diversify an organization are made to feel like "tokens." Sociologists' research on the experiences and strategies of women pioneers in previously all-male professions provides a useful parallel here. In her classic study of women in corporations, Rosabeth Moss Kanter argued that the proportion of women in an organization shapes how women are viewed and treated, and constrains or enables the ways that women can maneuver in the organization.[3] Kanter described organizations where the proportion of women was 15% or less as "skewed." Women in a "skewed" organization (and VFP likely is close to this in its proportion of women members) tend to suffer from

Figure 3.1 Army veteran Phoenix Johnson with Veterans For Peace "Arlington West" exhibit, 2019 VFP Convention, Spokane, WA
Photo by author

numerous disadvantages attached to tokenism, including lack of access to informal networks of support and advancement. Token women also find that they have very narrow avenues to survival, much less advancement to leadership, too often facing double-standards that disparage them for being "too masculine" if they speak and act assertively, or conversely, as not to be taken seriously if they dress or interact in ways that foreground their feminine attractiveness. Kanter argues that in "tilted" organizations, where the proportion of women was between 16% and 35% (and I would guess About Face is closer to this profile), women also often suffer disadvantages, but they at least have access to small networks of women co-workers, who potentially can offer support and become sources of informal mentoring. Sociologist Adia Harvey Wingfield's recent research on African American women's and men's experiences in previously White male dominated professions shows that gendered racism further narrows the eye of the needle for women and men of color tokens who are navigating careers in "skewed" organizations.[4]

Of course, VFP and About Face are not professional workplaces; they are social movement organizations founded on progressive views on race, class, and gender. But shared progressive values do not automatically eliminate the realities of tokenism. The first time I met Monique Salhab, in fact, they told me that "VFP has perfected the art of tokenism." Salhab had been startled when approached at the 2015 VFP national convention in Asheville and invited to run for a seat on the national VFP Board. "It was literally my first convention," Salhab recalls, and their first thought was, "You don't know me from Adam. You don't know about me. You don't know what I've done, what I could offer." Salhab was told flatly, "Oh, well, we are trying to recruit younger vets and women and people of color." Salhab decided to run, and their candidate statement on the 2016 VFP ballot included a brief overview of their military career, their social service and VFP chapter work in Albuquerque, the Buddhist roots of their commitments to peace, and this declaration of their positionality:

> I would be naïve to ignore the elements of how our society chooses to compartmentalize my existence via gender, race, sexuality, economic status, education, etc., so I acknowledge them. I identify as a queer woman of color. These labels are not important to me because I wish them to be, but because of how our society forces me to exist within its marginalized structure.[5]

Four years later, Salhab would make similar criticisms of how VFP's "marginalized structure" served to "compartmentalize [their] existence . . . as a queer woman of color." In retrospect, Salhab views their three years serving on the board as "overall positive," but was dismayed to find "a pattern of where women's voices were not amplified, were not given space. It is still a male organization. There is this male construct that exists, the way of thinking, the way of doing things, behaviors."

Monisha Ríos shared time on the board with Salhab, and her experience was similar. Ríos joined VFP in 2015, and it seemed almost immediately, "I got asked to join the board, kind of out of nowhere. And so I ran, and I got elected, which was a complete surprise to me, 'cause I'm nobody in Veterans For Peace at that point." In addition to sharing Salhab's experiences of being ignored or talked-over by other board members, Ríos was deeply disappointed at what she experienced as the continuing sexism in VFP. Initially, Ríos was enthused because those who recruited her to run agreed "that VFP should really turn its attention to sexual violence." When I asked her whether, as a member of the board, she had been able to move VFP toward addressing military sexual trauma, she sighed and replied,

> if I'm honest—and I am honest—it's not going so well. There's military cul-
> ture *in* VFP. We can't escape it. It's in us. There's the toxicity of it, of the
> hyper-masculinity that's there. And I wondered out loud, too, if it's because
> maybe we have some perpetrators among us. Who don't want to look at
> themselves. And I can understand that. I can have compassion for that, but
> at the same time, like, I'm sorry, but this isn't about you anymore. I have
> observed the [VFP] conversations around My Lai, focused on the massacre
> and the atrocity of it, but when it comes to actually talking about the rapes,
> we can't have that conversation. We can't talk about military sexual trauma,
> we can't talk about the issues of women veterans in Veterans For Peace. We
> have a MeToo movement in VFP. At both conventions I've been to, I've been
> groped. I was forced to kiss somebody, there is sexist stuff happening all the
> time. Women veterans in Veterans For Peace are constantly pushed aside,
> ignored, or tokenized and used to make VFP look diverse. When they're
> not inclusive.

The comments by Salhab and Ríos underline the central point of this chapter: how a progressive organization's commitment to *diversity*, expressed through sincere efforts to recruit women of color into leadership positions, can be undermined by its inability to be fully *inclusive* of these new members' concerns and perspectives.

Many longtime members of VFP recognize this problem. Vic, for instance, is a former board member who has worked to diversify VFP but is also con- fused by complaints of tokenism by Salhab, Ríos, and others. "People are complaining, and rightfully so, that it's an almost all White male organiza- tion, how do we become something else? Well, clearly one of the ways that we become something else is by putting some other kinds of people into lead- ership positions. But if they get to those leadership positions and feel like, well, 'We are just tokens here,' then how do you overcome that?" On the one hand, Vic sees that the purpose of diversifying the membership is more than to simply change appearances: "It's not because we want the board to *look* dif- ferent, it's because we want the board to *be* different." But on the other hand, he seems to put the onus for overcoming tokenism on the new members themselves: "If they feel like they are tokens they ought to prove, 'Hey, we are serious. So don't think we are tokens.'" In the end, Vic seems stumped: "It's a real dilemma. Damned if you do and damned if you don't."

In the remainder of this chapter, I will show how the yawning gap between VFP's commitment to diversity and its embrace of inclusivity is wedged apart, not by a lack of effort or seriousness from the newer members, but by systemic processes in the organization itself—processes with which About Face has begun to grapple more openly. As a frustrated Monisha Ríos summed up her VFP experience, "I repeatedly offered myself, offered my services, offered my experience, and I would get the patronizing, you know, 'Oh yeah, okay.' They want their little half brown Puerto Rican girl to make them look like they have diversity down. They're still ignoring our wisdom, our experience. It's just more erasure, more of 'you'll have to do things our way. We are inviting you into our space and you should be thankful for us that we're giving you the opportunities that we're giving you.' I've literally been told these things."

In what follows, I will point to systemic organizational processes— sometimes subtle, sometimes not so subtle—that marginalize and silence women, especially women of color and LGBTQ2S people: the valuing of narrow conceptions of military masculinity, which makes some people look like true leaders, and others less so; routine microaggressions targeted at women of color; and double standards that celebrate White men's expressions of passion, while viewing expressions of emotion from women and people of color negatively.

This is what a leader looks like

It was a heady time for anti-war activities in the years following 2004, when, fresh out of military prison, Stephen Funk dove in as a charter member of Iraq Veterans Against the War. The U.S. war in Iraq was escalating, as was the anti-war movement. Suddenly, Funk was in demand—as a speaker here, at a public demonstration there. He thrived as part of the "great momentum" of IVAW's growth and public presence. But Funk also noted with some dismay that the leadership of IVAW was made up of "a super majority of bros." Some of the same patterns he had found so oppressive in the marine corps— especially the escalation of hyper-masculine White men into positions of leadership—seemed to be reproducing themselves in IVAW.

I think that people fall into the habits of, "Oh, this is what a leader looks like." You see the same tall, White guys being the squad leaders again. I think people leave the military and they don't want to adopt those again, but then they go, "Oh, but I'm a leader! I'm a straight White guy. My voice is the loudest and I am the most important person here." Yeah, and so the women stay in the kitchen. And then for people who are gay [and] had experiences in the military, it's traumatizing to even just go back into that. People get frustrated when they get automatically put in those roles. It's like: we don't have to repeat these patterns. We can mix it up, right? We're against that, aren't we? Aren't we trying to work against that?

Army veteran Wendy Barranco joined IVAW a couple of years after Funk did, and her experience with leadership seems quite different. Working with a group of mostly men marine corps vets in Los Angeles as they launched anti-war educational events, initiated counter-recruitment efforts, and joined public demonstrations, Barranco rose to a position of leadership in the local chapter. "Surprisingly I work really well with marines. They are really great at taking orders [chuckles]. They listen well. And they are fucking effective. I really enjoyed working with them." How did it happen that this young woman veteran was able to lead this group of men vets? For one thing, it likely added to Barranco's veteran creds that she had served in a combat zone for nine months.[6] As Monisha Ríos had told to me, she learned early in VFP circles that "[i]f you weren't in combat you're nothing."

In retrospect, Wendy Barranco sees her IVAW leadership position between 2007–2009 as "an anomaly" in the larger national organization that was then led mostly by men. And she also now sees that it probably cemented the men's support as the group's leader that she shared a "singular focus" of ending the war with her men comrades, that she didn't think to press for the group to focus on issues related to gender or sexuality.

I didn't come into this work wearing race, class, gender glasses. That's something that evolved over time for me. When I first started doing that with the marines, it was very much about ending the war. I think a large part of why we worked well together in my opinion is because of that synergy, because we were very much on the same page about where our focus should lie and how we were going to go about doing it. Was it nuanced? Was it complex? Was it intersectional? Probably not. That's a fair critique. Probably not.

I was very young and green in my early activist days. It's only over time that I started gaining that analysis.

As we have seen, a more "nuanced" and "intersectional" analysis has been pushed to the center of internal discussions in About Face in recent years, and this has corresponded with Brittany DeBarros and other women and men of color assuming positions of national leadership. By contrast, VFP has recently experienced the excruciating false-start of recruiting women of color to the board, only to see them leave in frustration. In 2019, two relative newcomers to VFP—a woman of color whom I informally interviewed and Phoenix Johnson—told me that they had declined invitations to run for the national board, having heard words of caution from their more seasoned colleagues. Thus, at the 2019 national meeting, those who stepped forward and offered to run for the board were all men, most of them White, and most of them older.

Meanwhile, the escalation of White male combat veterans to positions of VFP leadership continued. In 2019, Garett Reppenhagen, an Iraq War army sniper, became the executive director and public face of VFP. Many members I spoke with expressed excitement at having a younger vet as the VFP leader, and they were encouraged that Reppenhagen stated his support for diversifying the membership and pledged to grapple with the internal schisms created by lingering sexism, racism, and homophobia. One woman of color I spoke with, however, was skeptical, seeing Reppenhagen as "just another basic bro with a big story." Another woman of color veteran said she appreciated Reppenhagen, but she wondered openly what his appointment meant for the future of VFP.

> Garrett is a great guy, but if you want to talk about the survival of our organization, if you want to talk about inclusion, right? Not just diversity, but also inclusion and belonging—*that's* your move? That's your move for executive director? And again, not to take credit away from his chops, but going back to situated knowledge, come on: you can't tell me that there wasn't a woman of color or a trans person, someone who could have led that organization, right?

Radical members of social movement organizations may hope—as Wendy Barranco does—that one day their organization will evolve to be fully democratic and leaderless. But for the time being, they face the pragmatic reality of choosing leaders who will be the face of the organization, when working with the public (including the mass media) and when working in coalition with other progressive movement organizations. Movement activists know that some members of the public and the mass media are likely to listen to and respect the words of a conventionally masculine White man who fits their ideal conception of what a combat veteran and a leader looks like. In *Some Men*, a book about men's participation in feminist anti-violence organizations, my colleagues and I called this "the pedestal effect"—the tendency for men, especially those who are tall, are athletic, and embody conventional masculine styles, to be viewed as respected heroes, escalated into positions of authority and public respect, to be listened to and "heard" when saying the same things that women have been saying for years.[7] If anything, veterans' peace organizations' decisions to escalate men with military masculine creds and to push them forward as public spokespeople, likely seems even more attractive: Just listen to what this guy says about the trauma of war and the need for peace— and he was an Army sniper![8] On the other hand, as I explore in subsequent chapters, continuing to push forward White men as the main public face of veterans' peace and justice organizations may slow the engagement with the internal work the organization needs to become truly inclusive, and may also impede the organization's ability to credibly forge intersectional alliances with non-veterans' social justice organizations.

For some of the younger veterans, the question of current and future leadership in About Face and VFP is, as Wendy Barranco put it, about White men "ceding power. For me that's the center of it. You've got to do something radical, and something radical is let women lead, period. Get out of the way. Bring women in. Capable women, and let them lead authentically, with executive power." Barranco concedes that "Especially for an organization like VFP, that's a lot to ask," particularly considering what she calls "the violence of tokenizing. You cannot sit here and talk about diversity and having women of color in the organization, and bring them into systems and environments that are really dangerous. We're talking about microaggressions, we're talking about possible sexual harassment. We're talking about all of those things that that are just another extension of the military."

Microaggressions and gaslighting

The first time I met Monique Salhab, we were sitting at a table having a coffee with two men VFP members. One of them, a White man in his 70s, was also meeting Salhab for the first time. He was delighted, it seemed, to learn that they were a VFP member. "You are a two-fer," he said to them cheerfully, "maybe even a three-fer." His comment—apparently referring to Salhab's being a woman, Black, and queer—was perhaps intended as a welcoming acknowledgment of their multiple identities. Salhab responded with a thin smile. The other guy at the table, a middle-aged Latino veteran, cringed and changed the subject. It struck me at the time that this sort of comment, however well intended, is often received as just another in a series of microaggressions[9] akin to those routinely absorbed by "minorities" who are viewed as beneficiaries of affirmative action "quotas" that improve the public face of an organization.

Research has shown how an accumulation of microaggressions— precisely because these seemingly small, perhaps even well-meaning, slights make one feel othered and marginalized—negatively impacts the physical and mental health of people from marginalized groups; death by a thousand cuts, as it were. Counseling psychologist Kevin L. Nadal and his colleagues found that an accumulation of microaggressions creates mental health challenges for people of color.[10] Medical researcher Melissa L. Walls and her research team found that the "unconscious biases" and "racial microaggressions" routinely faced by American Indians contributes to that population's poor health and lower life expectancy.[11] And research by social work scholar Kimberly F. Balsam and her colleagues provides evidence that "[l]esbian, gay, and bisexual individuals who are also racial/ethnic minorities (LGBT-POC) are a multiply marginalized population subject to microaggressions associated with both racism and heterosexism." The routine "multiple stressors" faced by this population, Balsam argues, can have devastating health impacts.[12]

In an organizational context, microaggressions can take the form of White men's and women's not listening to or not taking seriously the questions, analysis, or suggested strategies that women, people of color and LGBTQ2S people put on the table. In explaining her frustration in hitting a brick wall of indifference when proposing that VFP should expand its support for Puerto Rican veterans in the aftermath of the island's devastating 2017 earthquake, Monisha Ríos lamented, "If Noam Chomsky didn't write it, or if Dave Swanson didn't write it, or Anne Wright, or any of the people that they favor and look up to—who happen to also be White, and in a certain financial strata—they don't listen to it, they don't value it, or respect it or even try to understand it."

When a microaggression occurs, Monisha Ríos told me, she tries to think, "How can I use this as a teaching moment, that I'm trying to educate and empower the person giving the microaggression, so that they can understand what they're doing?" Sometimes, Ríos told me, "Those experiences are productive, we actually have some learning happen. And I get to experience empathy for them, they hopefully get to experience empathy for me." Too often, though, Ríos has found people in VFP circles "take immediate offense" at being called on their microaggressions, "because for them that automatically means a hood and a burning cross, or physical violence, and they don't really have an analysis of structural violence, or how microaggressions work." The recipient of a microaggression, therefore, has a decision to make in the moment: expend the energy necessary to make the event "a teaching moment," in the hope that it will result in an expansion of mutual empathy, and then be ready to deal with the exhausting and dispiriting negative fallout when the offender gets defensive; or, simply shine it on with no comment, absorb the insult, and deal with the accumulation of hurt and anger that results from a lifetime of small indignities.

Brittany DeBarros recalls witnessing sexist microaggressions the first time she visited a VFP chapter meeting. She was taken aback at being "40 years younger" than most of the others in the room, she recalls, but she was especially put off as she "sat and watched the men really disrespect" the only other woman in the room. In Debarros's view, the men "undermined her in ways that felt really familiar to me. It felt very familiar as a woman officer from the military, right?" This experience was part of the reason DeBarros decided to pour most of her energies into About Face. DeBarros values VFP and stays connected with the organization. Still, when it comes to the micro-dynamics of gendered racism, it seems that some VFP members just don't get it. DeBarros described for me the aftermath of her talk at the 2019 VFP meetings, where she spoke about how women of color veterans are too often "talked to" but are rarely asked about their experiences or their opinions.

After that panel, there was literally a line of old White men who just lined up and each of them spoke at me for five, ten each. Didn't ask a single question. And I was like, "I literally just talked about this." And it was just the irony of them being like, "I really like what you said," and then just ranting about their experiences with post 9/11 vets and going on and on. And none of those people had meant any harm. They were being—they were trying to be nice, trying to connect with me and I could see that. And yet I had just given advice about that very thing, and it was completely in one ear out the other.

Attempts by newcomers to create dialogue about microaggressions are sometimes met with "gaslighting," the tendency of people with more power to imply that the slights or microaggressions facing women or people of color are just in their heads, that they are misinterpreting the situation. There is not a great deal of research on gaslighting but in a recent study on domestic violence, sociologist Page L. Sweet shows how abusers use gaslighting to undermine their victims' confidence in their own interpretations of the violence they are experiencing. "Abusers mobilize gendered stereotypes," Sweet explains, as well as "structural vulnerabilities related to race, nationality, and sexuality, and institutional inequalities against victims to erode their realities."[13]

Gaslighting is deployed in organizational settings too, often against newcomers who may already be prone to doubt their own perspective, due in part to their social distance from those who have held power in the organization. Monisha Ríos said that she experienced gaslighting by VFP board members when she reported her own mistreatment from VFP members. "I reported a groping, and when someone forced me to kiss them at a convention. And one of the individuals on the board who happens to be a White male, said, 'Well I interpreted that differently.'"

Microaggressions in organizations are more than personally harmful; cumulatively, they form the interactional scaffolding that bolsters continued structural inequalities. So when victims of microaggressions "call in" perpetrators, they do so not simply to address their own hurt feelings; they do so to move the organization toward equality in gender and race relations. Yet, the emotional burden of having to be the one to confront perpetrators every time they commit a microaggression, and the cumulative exhaustion of having to endure gaslighting when one does, points to the cost of placing the burden of change on individual victims. Instead, younger veterans are pressing their organizations to engage in critical internal dialogue about microaggressions and gaslighting. There is another issue that prevents such a discussion from proceeding in a fully productive way: how gendered racism in organizations shapes emotions, and peoples' interpretations and responses to others' expression of emotions.

His passion, her hysteria

Emotions—particularly anger and moral outrage over injustices—have long fueled progressive social movements. The massive 2020 street demonstrations across the United States in response to police violence against Black people offer a stunning example of this. Some who witness the raised fists, thunderous crowd clamor, or the bursts of anger that sometimes erupt during huge street protests see only aberrant bedlam. But in a foundational 1981 article, Peter Lyman argued against the notion of anger as irrational; rather, he pointed to anger as a necessary and productive foundation for progressive action.[14] That same year, in a stirring keynote speech on "The Uses of Anger" delivered to the National Women's Studies Association, Audre Lorde directly confronted White feminists' fears of Black women's anger, pointing to its productive necessity in confronting racism.

> My response to racism is anger. I have lived with that anger, ignoring it, feeding upon it, learning to use it before it laid my visions to waste, for most of my life. Once I did it in silence, afraid of the weight. My fear of anger taught me nothing. Your fear of that anger will teach you nothing, also. Women responding to racism means women responding to anger; Anger of exclusion, of unquestioned privilege, of racial distortions, of silence, ill-use, stereotyping, defensiveness, misnaming, betrayal, and co-optation.[15]

More recently, sociologist James Jasper has challenged dualistic—mind/body, rational/emotional—understandings of what drives social movements, introducing the awkward term "feeling-thinking processes" to capture the productive fusion of rational calculation and moral outrage in protest movements.[16]

As scholars increasingly recognize emotions as an essential aspect of protest, they also point to the ways in which emotional expressions like anger and outrage are read and responded to differently, based on who is expressing them. In his study of the animal rights movement, Julian McAllister Groves observes that men activists are applauded and admired for expressing emotion—be it anger or tears—and are often subsequently escalated to positions as leaders and public spokespeople. Women's expressions of compassion for animals, conversely, is too often interpreted as reflecting their irrationality.[17] Similarly, sociologist Verta Taylor's research on feminist and LGBTQ2S movements has recognized both the importance of emotion in these movements, and the ways that gendered double-standards concerning emotions have created challenges for women activists.[18] Men, for instance, have frequently discounted women's expressions of anger or outrage, claiming that their views are irrational, clouded by their being "overly emotional." As we saw earlier, when Monisha Ríos raised her voice to be heard in a VFP board meeting, she learned later that behind her back another board member was labeling her as "unstable." By contrast, Ríos said, when an older man gets loud or excited in a VFP meeting, he's viewed as "passionate." And if he should cross a line with bullying and aggression, the behavior is often excused and minimized by others who attribute it "to his PTSD." Women veterans, as we have seen, also commonly suffer from PTSD, their military sexual trauma in particular often fueling lasting struggles with depression, but it appears that the existence of internalized trauma does not normally draw women veterans a pass when they express anger.[19]

The gendered double-standard concerning emotions in veterans' peace organizations echoes a rational man/emotional woman dichotomy that has long been built into Western societies and is amplified in military culture. As Cynthia Enloe has written, "Militarization legitimizes masculinized men as protectors, as actors, as rational strategists, while it places feminized people in the role of emotionally informed, physically weak, only parochially aware protected."[20] The recent surge of women into the U.S. military, including into combat zones, sometimes as officers, challenges this neat dichotomy. And women veterans' entry into previously mostly-male veterans' peace organizations lays bare the lingering echoes of this gendered double-standard in progressive spaces: Women expressing anger are "unstable"; men are "passionate."

This gendered asymmetry also echoes a deeper cultural pattern of women's emotional upsets being viewed as emanating from their supposedly biological tendencies toward irrationality and emotional fragility. "Hysteria," writes historian Cecilia Taska, "is undoubtedly the first mental disorder attributable to women, accurately described in the second millennium BC, and until Freud considered an exclusively female disease."[21] There is a historical irony to the current gendered ways that PTSD in some contexts today serves as an excuse for men who act out in angry, bullying, or even violent ways. According to historian George Mosse, during World War I, soldiers' symptoms of "shell shock" (a precursor to the clinical PTSD diagnosis created during the Vietnam War) was viewed as a kind of "enfeebled manhood," related to hysteria in women.[22]

This sexist double-standard in expressions of emotion tends to be amplified when the loud or angry woman in question is a woman of color. Research by sociologist Adia Harvey Wingfield shows that gendered racism in workplaces tends to create a different set of "feeling rules" for Black people, compared with Whites.[23] Phoenix Johnson, for instance, pointed to instances when White people benefitted from crying in progressive spaces. Once, when a White man leader whom Johnson came to see as marginally competent wept in a meeting, people seemed to fall all over themselves praising his tears: "They're like, 'Oh! He's, such a great guy! Oh, he's in touch with his feelings!' [laughs] But then they look at me as my stereotype as just a stupid Indian, and I'm like, well, this guy can't even fucking spell." On other occasions, Johnson was frustrated when witnessing how "the tears of White women" in About Face or VFP meetings garnered sympathy and a listening ear from others, especially White men.

White women's tears, Johnson said, are an example of what anti-racism educator Catrice M. Jackson calls "weapons of whiteness."[24] In veterans' contexts, Phoenix Johnson experienced White women's tears as just another microaggression that harmed and silenced women of color. "Some of these White women are really good at crying. They turn it into a personal issue: 'Oh, you just have a personal issue with me. It really hurts my feelings that you are saying this.' Well, it really hurts my existence that you're being racially oppressive. They make it all about them and their feelings. That fragility gets weaponized for sure. They beckon the attention of the White males." Sociologist Robin DiAngelo devotes a full book chapter to discussing the sources, meaning, and impact of "tears shed by White women in cross-racial settings," as an especially "pernicious enactment of White fragility." Especially in progressive settings, White women's tears create an opening for White men to assume a patriarchal posture of rescuing the weeping woman, DiAngelo observes. "While she is given attention, the people of color are yet again abandoned and/or blamed."[25]

For older men in VFP, a certain level of hostility in meetings might just seem normal, like business as usual. In fact, the sociologist DiAngelo says that while in cross-racial settings, White women may express White fragility with tears, White men's fragility "most commonly shows up as varying forms of dominance and intimidation."[26] Responding to my question about women of color's complaints of bullying and abuse by VFP men, longtime VFP member Vic said, "It's funny, because the business about men yelling at board members, I think I told you, the first board that I met on—they were terrific people—but everything short of fistfights breaking out at board meetings and threatening to throw chairs at one another. Okay, that's the way these guys are." These behaviors may have seemed normal in the past—"that's the way these guys are"—but newcomers, especially women of color, experience these behaviors as harmful, and they see interpretive double-standards about the meanings of emotional outbursts as detrimental and unacceptable forms of gendered racism. Monique Salhab expressed this clearly: "I think there's this acceptance of men, and I witnessed it so many times in board meetings, where men are yelling at each other, threatening each other, and it's, 'Oh, well, he, he gets angry a lot. Just give him a few minutes, he'll cool down.'" On the other hand, Salhab said, she was on a phone call with other board members "[w]hen Monisha's mental status was questioned," and Salhab recalls feeling "a deep, deep pain, and I was so angry, so angry that a man, a White man would do that. Because the levels of anger that I had witnessed on the board from men, no one ever questioned their mental capacity, you know?"

Echoing Salhab and others, Brittany DeBarros says it is time for progressive organizations to recognize and end this emotional double-standard. "We let [White men] act however the fuck they want because we don't want to be mean to them because they have trauma, right? That's been the story for a really long time in veterans' spaces, and that prioritizes the comfort of people with dominant identities over women, queer folks, trans folks, right?" About Face has opened space for a critical discussion of these issues, DeBarros observed. And she wonders, along with others, whether recent cracks in the organizational edifice of VFP might open such a space for dialogue in that organization as well.

Confronting "a pattern across the field"

The microaggressions, gaslighting, emotional double-standards, and silencing of women of color's voices and leadership is not just a problem in veterans' peace and justice organizations, Brittany DeBarros told me. It's "a pattern across the field" of non-profit and other progressive movement organizations. Phoenix Johnson experienced this pattern when attending a leadership workshop for young veterans of color at the Highlander Center, the Tennessee institution famed for educating generations of progressive community leaders. Johnson was stoked, initially, to be participating a workshop with the goal of "empowering women of color." But early on, it began to feel "very patronizing."

And as the group moved toward developing a strategic plan for the mock action that would conclude their week together, Johnson and other vets of color were "shoved to the side" by the facilitator, "a White male, a very prototypical vision of the bleeding heart for veterans—like a six-foot tall, army infantry, maybe slightly conventionally pretty White male, and he's like, 'Okay, so I'm the leader of this group now, and I'm facilitating our final plan.'" The group's rhetoric about "empowering women of color," Johnson concluded, was largely "performative."

Women of color have challenged this "performative" commitment to diversity in many progressive organizations in recent years. In early 2019, Brittany DeBarros and others penned "[a]n open letter on the systemic mistreatment of womxn of color in social justice spaces," a message targeted to Common Defense—an anti-Trump veterans' organization with some membership overlap with About Face. The letter proclaimed "Time's Up" on the organization's systemic tokenism, gaslighting, and other processes that marginalize women of color.[27] At roughly the same time, DeBarros and Krystal Littlejohn, an Indigenous veteran activist, ascended to staff leadership positions with About Face. At first, DeBarros says, "We had a really hard time and were really gaslit and undermined in passive aggressive ways." But after some intense dialogue, DeBarros and Littlejohn received a vote of confidence and support from the About Face leadership. This left DeBarros feeling optimistic about the immediate future of About Face, which in her view, "consistently throughout its history has chosen evolution over falling into just accepting the toxicity and the problems that exist."

As her optimism for About Face grows, DeBarros remains skeptical, but constructively engaged with VFP. She told her VFP allies, "I'm committed to working with you and I believe in you as people," but she is doubtful about that organization's future, fearing that "the collective practice is not there to maintain trust." Monique Salhab would agree about the challenges facing VFP, particularly the question of whether some of the longstanding members of VFP are feeling displaced from their positions of centrality in the organization. Pressing for a deeper discussion of gendered racism within VFP resulted in Salhab receiving several "angry, angry, belligerent emails from men. And, I am not a White man but I do recognize that there is a level of fear—that you're reacting like this because you feel like somehow your power is being taken." With this comment, Salhab placed a finger on a point made by sociologist William J. Goode in his widely reprinted 1980 article, "Why Men Resist."[28] Goode observed that some men's (and we could extend his observation to some *White* men's) negative overreactions to recent social gains made by women were an example of what happens when a person is nudged away, even if just a bit, from their unexamined sense of entitlement to being at the center of social life—including the experience of being listened to and respected as a knowledgeable leader.

Some VFP men, though, seem to be listening, and critically examining their organization in light of stories they have been hearing from women of color members. Joe, for instance, told me that the women's stories—especially those of being sexually violated, harassed, or bullied by senior members of VFP—were a surprise to him: "I had no idea all of this shit was going on. All of a sudden, it just popped because Monique and Monisha spoke about it. And it was like, we have members who are pulling this crap? It was like poison in the well." Santiago had heard the women's stories before and had developed a deeper analysis of the behaviors of some of his VFP comrades:

We're for peace as an organization. And we're pushing against imperialism and colonialism. Yeah, but we've got our own imperialism and colonialism, and sexism within Veterans For Peace. Like at Spokane and back in St. Paul, when you have women having to endure sexist remarks, groping, suggestive bullshit, obviously we're not as progressive as we want to portray ourselves.

One barrier to About Face's or VFP's engaging in the critical internal work of confronting and changing their own internal sexism and racism is the view that some members have about the need to remain focused on "the mission"—narrowly defined as opposing militarization and promoting peace. Monique Salhab saw some VFP members' literal attachments to 'the organization's mission statement as akin to "fundamentalist Christians' " adherence to "the word of the Bible as it is written. There's no other interpretation. It's the mission statement as it's written. It's sort of that military mind, right? It's like, 'You've got the mission. There it is. That's it. There's no room for anything else.' "

Post 9/11 veterans told me a number of stories of frustration when their ideas or concerns bumped up against this sort of fundamentalist adherence to "the mission." Monisha Ríos uttered an exasperated laugh as she recalled more than one occasion when she and others shared their experiences of gendered racism in VFP, "Where this White woman will stand up and say, 'I don't see the point in addressing the problems of the movement,'—[laughs]— 'We're busy trying to build solidarity.' And then the rest of us are like, 'You really just said you're trying to build solidarity? By silencing us?'" Phoenix Johnson recalled with anger a time, when speaking to a White man About Face member on the phone, when Johnson raised issues of how racism had impacted Native people, "He says, 'The anti-war movement has absolutely nothing to do with Native people.'" I asked Johnson, "How do you respond to that?" Johnson replied, "You hang up."

The veterans' anti-war movement seems to be at an important juncture. A younger, diverse cohort of veterans has entered the movement, bringing a promising situated knowledge of the connections between militarism and war with racism, sexism, and homophobia. If members are willing to do the difficult, internal work of engaging in conversations about their own organizations, there is a possibility that these conversations will not only build greater inclusiveness and solidarity within the organizations, but as we will see in the next chapter, the centering of the new members' intersectional standpoints also promises to connect and integrate veterans' peace organizations with broad, progressive coalitions. If, on the other hand, the VFP can't or won't engage in this critical conversation about their own internal dynamics, it is possible that members like Barranco, DeBarros, Funk, Johnson, Ríos, and Salhab will decide to move on, to "just hang up."

***

In this chapter, I have shown how a younger, diverse generation of veterans has entered the veterans' peace movement, bringing with them a collective situated knowledge of the interconnectedness of militarism and war with race, gender, and sexual oppression. This intersectional knowledge situates this new cohort of activists to see and experience the previously normalized internal dynamics of progressive organizations like Veterans For Peace— particularly their everyday expressions of gendered racism—as oppressive and marginalizing for women, people of color, and queer people. The younger members have "called in" longtime veteran activists—many of them men, many of them White—to critical internal dialogue, with the goal of changing the internal dynamics and leadership of the veterans' peace movement. The longtime members' situated knowledge—politically radical, but also grounded in their collective experience as mostly White, heterosexual men—is expressed in sincere efforts to build diversity in the veterans' peace movement. But the fact that these members' situated knowledge is shaped by experiences of White and male privilege means that too often, the full inclusion sought by the younger members is impeded by the older members' expressions of (or toleration of others') gender and racial microaggressions, gaslighting, assumptions about what a real leader should look like, and their narrow views of what "the mission" of veterans' peace organizations should be.

In the next chapter, I move from this internal examination of veterans' peace organizations to a critical examination of their connections with other progressive organizations. Here too, I show that the newer members' intersectional praxis points the way toward an expansive and more fluid engagement with coalition politics.

Interlude 3

"We cannot stand in fear"

*Monique Salhab appears as a representative of Veterans For Peace,
June 6, 2020, on the weekly "Your New Mexico Government" podcast,
speaking during the height of the COVID pandemic and the national
uprisings over the police murder of George Floyd in Minneapolis.*[1]

Ekulona: I'm your host, Khalil Ekulona. While learning to adjust to life
during a global pandemic, the killing of George Floyd at the hands of
Minneapolis police officers has given rise to protests globally. Here with
me to talk about the heavy lifting all of us have to do is Monique Salhab.
[Salhab] is working with the Veterans For Peace. Monique, how does one
navigate the pandemic as well as the civil unrest? How are you holding on
with these things?

Salhab: I am trying to stay in a constant state of awareness of just where
my body is and how my body is feeling. So often we get disconnected
from our bodies and our minds. And I think especially over the last few
months, it's been even easier, with the suffering that we're witnessing and
those in our communities are experiencing. And then obviously with the
unfortunate, violent death of George Floyd—physically, viscerally feeling
that. And then just the overwhelming need to go into action.

Ekulona: And you served in the military. What branch did you serve?

Salhab: I served both in the air force and the army ten years, and then two
tours in Iraq.

Ekulona: Wow. So let me ask you, as a military veteran and you see these issues happening—police violence and the militarization of the police—as
a veteran, as someone who has fought and defended this country, yet you
see the injustices that take place at home, what type of perspective can
you offer to our listeners who may not see that?

Salhab: Since 9/11, we have systematically watched across the country, police departments become militarized. They have the equipment, they
have the weapons and their training has been modified to be more militaristic. And so, the death of George Floyd, when I watched that video,
and I watched that officer, and he killed him, now we should be wanting

justice for George Floyd's death, and for his family, and wanting to hold the police officer accountable. But we don't have that same outrage when it comes to the military. No one arrested me when I came home, but we say, "Oh, well, you were just doing your job." Well, guess what? The officers involved would argue "We were just doing our jobs." So as I watched National Guardsmen across our country, I recognized that wearing a uniform, whether it's a police uniform or military uniform, they don't say this explicitly, but you were taught to dehumanize. In order to dehumanize another human being you have to dehumanize yourself first.

Ekulona: Talk to me about navigating the anger that people are feeling, but at the same time, there is a global pandemic that's going around that's already made it dangerous to be outside.

Salhab: I think the beauty of what we're seeing, not only here in our own community in Albuquerque, but obviously across the country and on a global level, is that there's a deeper realization of wanting better. Knowing that we as human beings in our communities, especially being Black, Indigenous, people of color, that we deserve better. As individuals, we are willing to put our lives on the line. Like, yes, our lives are on the line literally every day, pre-COVID. The pandemic is an added complexity, but it's not stopped people from recognizing that we must fight for justice. We must fight to raise the truth of what George Floyd's death symbolized. And prior to his death, there was already the stripping away of any levels of denial about the inequities to our systems, the healthcare system, the education system, and so on and so forth. And to me, we cannot stand in fear. And I look at what folks are doing with their fear is that they are mobilizing, they're turning it into an action-oriented energy.

4

"Connecting the dots"

From movement silos to intersectional coalitions

A towering steel fence separates Tijuana and San Diego, extending like a scar into the Pacific Ocean. For more than a quarter century, just before Christmas, people have gathered on each side of the fence to celebrate *La Posada Sin Fronteras*,[1] singing, praying, extending their hands and gifts of food through the narrow openings between the wall's unyielding bars. The annual ritual, according to sociologist Pierrette Hondagneu-Sotelo, is "an interfaith, predominantly Christian, celebration of cross-border unity and protest against the social injustices of U.S. border policies."[2] As the 25th anniversary of *La Posada Sin Fronteras* approached in late 2018, the escalating cruelties of U.S. treatment of Central American and Mexican migrants and asylum-seekers—including the separation of families and the caging of children—deepened the sense of urgency for those pressing for more humanitarian policies. The U.S. Customs and Border Protection (CBP) further escalated the crisis by announcing that *Posada* celebrants on the U.S. side would be required this year to remain at least 60 meters from the fence.

On December 16, 2018, over 400 people on the U.S. side of the border gathered to speak, pray, and protest the inhumane treatment of migrants and the escalating militarization of the border. When the group processed to the wall, they were met by a line of CBP agents in riot gear, who commanded them to disperse. The protestors, mostly interfaith clergy, joined by two U.S. military combat veterans wearing About Face t-shirts, held their ground. Hands raised, with open-palms facing forward in the now-familiar "don't shoot" posture of peaceful protestors, Wendy Barranco knelt in the sand with a first row of protestors, as Brittany DeBarros stood directly behind her with others (Figure 4.1). The 32 of those who refused to be moved were arrested. Four of them, including Barranco and DeBarros, rejected a guilty plea, forcing a trial.

What brought two anti-war veterans to a direct action for migrant justice at the border? It turns out that Wendy Barranco—who had herself migrated from Mexico to Southern California as a child—had in recent months been

Unconventional Combat. Michael A. Messner, Oxford University Press. © Oxford University Press 2021.
DOI: 10.1093/oso/9780197573631.003.0004

Figure 4.1 About Face members Wendy Barranco and Brittany Ramos
DeBarros protest injustice to migrants, Mexico–U.S. border, December 16, 2018
© REUTERS/Carlos Garcia Rawlins

using the skills she had learned as a combat medic in Iraq to help staff a medical clinic for migrants and local Mexicans in Tijuana. But this, the border protest, was "a separate action" from her humanitarian medical work, Barranco told me. While in Phoenix, Arizona, for a Veterans Organizing Institute event, she had encountered some other vets who told her about the upcoming protest at the border, organized by the American Friends Service Committee and the Poor People's Campaign. "I said, 'Well, sounds interesting, sounds like a good opportunity to disrupt.' So Brittany and I decided, 'Let's do it,' you know?"

For her part, Brittany DeBarros was still deeply enmeshed with her legal struggle with the U.S. Army, waiting to learn if she would be court-martialed or discharged. The previous month she had joined veterans in Philadelphia to protest former Vice President Joe Biden's presentation of the Liberty Medal to former President George W. Bush. DeBarros had also recently become active with the Poor People's Campaign, and she had been barnstorming around the U.S. with "Drop the MIC," About Face's effort to facilitate public discussions about the human and financial costs of the Military Industrial Complex. One of these costs, DeBarros knew, was the militarization of the U.S.–Mexico border, recently escalated by the Trump administration. Standing up for migrants at the border, for DeBarros, meshed neatly with these efforts to address poverty, institutionalized racism, and militarism.

Following a non-violent arrest training with the Quakers, Barranco and DeBarros learned from the organizers that the plan was to hold a rally, and then those who had decided in advance "to engage in civil disobedience" would together "walk straight up to the wall." Recently, they learned, the CBP had been laying down coils of concertina razor wire to prevent access to the wall from the U.S. side. They had also heard, Barranco told me, that U.S. authorities were "cancelling *La Posada Sin Fronteras*" that had been held there for years, most likely, she concluded, "to be cruel. I mean, cruelty is the point of this administration, besides making money."

"CBP immediately came out in full battle rattle," Barranco recalled, "full riot gear ready to take us down." When the protestors sat down and sang, "it was a standoff. It was tense. It's very tense. And it felt a lot like deployment—the same kind of rush and feel—in that moment, realizing that that is where I needed to be at that point in time. So our resolve was just, 'We're not moving.'" Eventually the CBP moved forward, started "to push us, and they began to maneuver to start arresting us." The roughness with which each arrestee was treated was correlated, in Barranco's view, with race: "The Reverend's got a knee on his back, his mouth was in the sand. The Imam, same thing. Just treated like dirt. And somehow a lot of the White women, a lot of the White dudes, unscathed. Unscathed."

Most of those arrested pled guilty and accepted a small fine. But Barranco told the others, "It doesn't feel right to me to plead guilty. This is bullshit. It's a bullshit charge. We have every right to be down there. And frankly, I think we could organize around this, bring more attention to migrant justice." DeBarros and two religious leaders agreed. The charges that were eventually brought against the four, "Failure to obey a federal officer's directions," were, in Barranco's view, "ridiculous." The four knew that they "didn't have two nickels to rub together," but their defense coalesced through "a sense of synergy when good people come together, and they want to collaborate on something that's right and truthful and just." DeBarros mobilized a GoFundMe effort through About Face for the four's legal defense. A handful of attorneys worked the case pro-bono. At one point the four were offered a deal to settle, but they refused, seeing it as an opportunity to "put the government on trial" for "violations of human rights at the border."[3] The following October, 2019, the four were acquitted. Both before and after the trial, Barranco said, they worked to promote a line of argument about U.S. policy:

> A point that I think Brit did really well at advancing is, why are *we* on trial? This colonizer government should be on trial for crimes against humanity at the border. People are waiting months and months for asylum. They're being denied. Just the absurdity of the "law and order" argument, right? We tried to advance a narrative of turning that on its head, of like, "This is the court that has power: the people's court, and it's you the colonizer who's is guilty." I think we made it a point that day. But I mean, to me personally it was hard to be happy about a win when there's still people and kids in cages.

The story of Barranco's and DeBarros's 2018–2019 border action, arrest, and acquittal encapsulates the main themes of this chapter. In what follows, I show how the situated knowledge of the younger cohort of veterans who are the focus of this book leads them to see and build organic intersectional connections between the anti-militarism focus of About Face or Veterans For Peace, with work being done by organizations opposing racism and sexism, promoting justice for Indigenous Peoples and migrants, doing community health organizing at the border and in poor communities of color during the COVID-19 pandemic, and stopping climate change. Some of the skills they learned in the military, and much of the knowledge they have gained about militarization in their work with About Face and VFP, are resources that they bring to broad coalitions for social justice.

Quandaries of coalition-building

Younger activists frequently express their impatience with single-issue causes, preferring instead to build coalitions capable of intersectional action. But millennials did not invent coalition-building. Like many longstanding progressive organizations, Veterans For Peace has engaged in coalition politics with various national and international organizations for decades.[4] And since its inception, About Face has sought to ally with an array of peace groups and other progressive organizations. But like all progressive social movement organizations, VFP and About Face confront a built-in quandary: To what extent should they maintain a singular focus on the issue that is the raison d'etre of the organization (in this case opposing militarism and war), and to what extent should they nurture connections with progressive organizations with different foci?

Sociologist James Jasper has called this organizational quandary "the extension dilemma." On the one hand, keeping a tightly defined singular focus helps an organization maintain a distinct collective identity (we are veterans; we are for peace), and serves as a clear focal point for the organization's actions (we protest and educate against war and militarism). But when the organization is too rigid in maintaining its singular focus, it sets limits on the number of people who might join, and it also risks becoming so insular—so "siloed," in today's parlance—that it becomes irrelevant in the larger landscape of progressive politics. Additionally, there is the longstanding problem of singular organizations privileging the particular oppressions of their own constituents—say, the working class, or women, or Blacks—while treating other forms of inequality as of secondary importance, or ignoring them altogether.[5] At the other extreme, if an organization's boundaries become entirely porous, too fluid in its connections with other organizations, it risks losing its identity and its sense of purpose. As Jasper puts it, "The further you expand your group (or alliance), the less coherent your goals and actions can be . . . Furthermore, as potential power or reach increases, so do coordination problems."[6]

The extension dilemma is not an either-or prospect for movement organizations; rather, the quandary of how much to stay singularly focused versus how much to extend into coalition work presents organizations with an ongoing continuum of strategic choice. I observed a general tendency among veterans in VFP and About Face: Older and predominantly White and male veterans tend to lean toward maintaining a clear focus on war and peace in their work, while as much as possible showing up in support of others' efforts to address racism, class exploitation, colonialism, and climate change. By contrast, the younger and more diverse post-9/11 veterans tend to lean into intersectional action, strategically connecting their anti-militarism work in the organic ebb-and-flow of progressive organizing against racism, border injustice, or climate change. As Phoenix Johnson told me about the discussions taking place with their Seattle VFP chapter, "I mean, literally every single intersection, there's relevance when talking about the environment, women's rights, capitalism, racism. I mean, you name it, we're talking about." The younger activists' focus on these sorts of connections sometimes leads to strained relations with some older members who might prefer keeping a tighter, more singular focus. Monique Salhab expressed frustration

good explanation of VFP
ambivalence about SOA organizing

with how "there's confusion at times" among some VFP members when issues are raised that are not obviously related directly to war and peace.

> I think there's some who get it. And then I think there are those who are, "Oh, this is a distraction." One of the things that I remember [former VFP Executive Director] Michael McPherson talking about was "peace at home, peace abroad." That so resonated to me because there's truth in that. And, I remember just hearing people mumbling in the audience, some folks, "Oh, yeah," and other folks were, "Why do we need to talk about what's going on in a neighborhood when we should be talking about the war going on in Iraq?"

The tendency among the younger veterans to, in Salhab's words, analytically "connect the dots" between anti-militarism and community-based economic or racial justice issues is expressed in a nimbleness in their organizing tendencies. Younger activists tend to move quickly toward a current movement flashpoint—as did DeBarros and Barranco during the 2018–2019 migrant crisis at the border, and as did Monique Salhab and others during the eruption of racial justice activism in the spring of 2020. As I show in this chapter, the power of this flexible, intersectional action lies largely in the particular skills and knowledge that veterans can bring to these other struggles—for instance, how DeBarros and Barranco used their status as combat veterans to foreground a critical analysis of militarization in U.S. border politics.

This fluid strategic activism, on the other hand, introduces its own strains and challenges, three of which will emerge in my discussion. First, younger activists' emphasis on "connecting the dots" between different issues and struggles may be promising for movement coalition-building, but for individual activists it introduces a high potential for burnout, as a relatively small core of activists continually migrate from this action to that struggle, often with minimal financial support from their organizations. The relatively young activists that I focus on in this book each expressed to me their periodic sense of exhaustion with the depth and range of activism they felt compelled to engage in. Seen this way, some longtime VFP activists' narrower focus makes sense as a strategy to hang in there for the long haul. "You'd go crazy if you tried to do everything," I was told by an older White male VFP member who for years has focused his activism on maintaining "Arlington West," a sea of crosses his VFP chapter sets up each Sunday at the beach in Santa Monica, California, representing soldiers and others killed in the wars in Afghanistan and Iraq—and spending the day distributing VFP literature and talking with tourists and passers-by about the costs of war and the promise of peace.[7] Another longtime VFP member, who concentrates his energies on working for veterans' health issues, chose a military metaphor to describe his decades-long focus: "You can't fight the whole war yourself; you gotta' choose your trench and hunker down and fight there."

A second strain in veterans' engaging with a range of coalitional activism lies in *how* activists go about doing this work. The VFP members have long adopted a strategy of showing up, wearing VFP gear and waiving their massive white and black VFP banners, in support of protests or marches organized by other progressive groups. The VFP chapters will also frequently "table" at community events, distributing literature and opening conversations with members of the public. Some younger veterans in VFP and About Face are impatient with these tactics, sometimes even disparaging VFP members' "always showing up with their banners," at others' events. Especially critical in the eyes of women of color and LGBTQ2S activist veterans is the need to avoid assuming leadership when one joins another organization in coalition. As I show, the younger veterans have been critical of how, in their view, older White male VFP members impose a "White Savior" approach, especially when they join in support of efforts of Indigenous movements in the United States or abroad.

A final strain that is introduced by younger vets' tendency to engage in more fluid intersectional activism may ultimately lay bare the limits of VFP and About Face as distinct organizations, raising questions about their future in the larger ecology of progressive social movement activism. Some of the younger activists may eventually decide that VFP, and even the younger and more flexible About Face, are too singular in their focus, too rigid or slow in their ability to support the kinds of fluid activism they see as necessary in today's social movements' context. Wendy Barranco, for instance, appreciated the support she and DeBarros received from About Face during their direct action at the border. But she also began to wonder: Has she "outgrown" the "veterans' space" of About Face, and might she be more effective just working on her own?

I think a lot of organizations like to talk about doing work, but there's no follow-through, or it's really slow to get there. Orgs are typically not agile or flexible. I think About Face has talked about border work and border work and border work. And it's like, okay, but I'm *already doing* border work. The question you should be asking I think is, "how do I support your border work?" I'm already here, I'm already doing it. From my Facebook and social media, I just raise funds on my own and get my ass down there on my own and do the work on my own.

Anti-racism and anti-poverty work

In the spring of 2020, sparked by the police killing of George Floyd, massive protests for racial justice erupted—first in Minneapolis, then in cities and towns across the United States, and eventually across the globe. Initially, many people were surprised at the size and scope of the uprisings, and also with the multiracial composition of the Black-led protests. As weeks of protest continued, it became increasingly apparent that institutions—from universities, to mass media, to cities and the U.S. military—were bending to the movement's demands for anti-racist change, including police reform, re-prioritized city budgets, and the tearing down of public monuments that commemorated racist leaders of the past.

George Floyd was one in a long and violent history of Black people killed by police, so why and how did this movement grow so quickly, spread so widely, and apparently achieve a deeper public and institutional response than did similar racist killings and subsequent protests? Part of the answer may lie in the timing of this event, coming as it did during the depths of the COVID-19 pandemic that had laid bare how the combined health and financial crisis disproportionately hurt Indigenous and poor people, Blacks, immigrants, and others who were already living on the edge of precarity. But the breadth and impact of the 2020 racial justice movement was also due to the years of savvy organizing and public education by Black Lives Matter, the Poor People's Campaign, and other organizations, much of it below the public radar. This organizational groundwork laid foundations in consciousness-raising about institutional racism, and strategically developed the leadership and the coalitional connections that made possible the eventual uprisings and their aftermath.

Commentators pointed to continuity with past racial justice movements, while noting the ways that the 2020 uprising expressed new and different dimensions. Drawing from the words of historian Tyree Boyd-Pates, an *LA Times* analysis concluded that "[t]he current movement for Black lives, scholars assert, is more intersectional than any of its predecessors and includes more women in leadership roles, as well as members of the LGBTQ community. Black queer women, in particular, deserve credit for the Black Lives Matter movement."[8] Indeed, the spring 2020 racial justice demonstrations were multi-generational, multi-racial, and multi-gender—in a word, intersectional—highlighted, for instance, by the massive June 14, 2020, "All Black Lives Matter" march in Los Angeles, organized by Black LGBTQ+ Activists for Change.[9]

About Face and VFP were also quick to support the 2020 racial justice uprisings. In June, when President Donald Trump ordered troops to use teargas to forcibly clear peaceful protestors from a park in front of the White House, so that he could stage a photo-op waiving a Bible in front of a church, and when he threatened to send military troops into cities and states that refused to treat protestors with similar force, About Face and VFP issued public calls to National Guard and other troops to "stand down for Black lives," should they be ordered to engage in violence against citizens engaged in peaceful protest (Figure 4.2). In addition, over 700 veterans signed an About Face open letter, "urging activated National Guard troops to do the right thing and refuse to help in suppressing righteous protest demanding racial justice."[10] About Face and VFP members also joined Black Lives Matter protests throughout the nation, and members joined in several online town halls and forums about racial justice.

About Face and VFP members have long been connected with anti-racism efforts in the United States. When I interviewed VFP member Daniel Craig in 2016 for *Guys Like Me*, the Latino Gulf War veteran was wearing a t-shirt emblazoned with "Black Lives Matter" across the chest, and "Veterans For Peace" in smaller script below. I asked him if there was a Black Lives Matter–VFP coalition in his town of Santa Fe, New Mexico, a place with very few Blacks, and he replied, "It's an alignment. We're all working toward basically common cause. We've aligned with different groups in support of the Black Lives Matter movement." He then noted that VFP also had recently enacted a national effort, partly in response to the rise of Donald Trump, to oppose Islamophobia. These sorts of alignments, Craig explained, were an effort at "finding common cause" with other groups, connected with VFP's emphasis on war and peace. "Basic human rights. Basic human dignity. For VFP, our forte is military issues. The veterans' experience. It's woven into Black Lives Matter, countering Islamophobia . . . racism, sexism, the LGBTQ community's persecution. They all weave into human rights."

Figure 4.2 About Face "Troops Stand Down for Black Lives" campaign, June 2020

© Aaron Hughes, 2020

African American veteran of the Iraq War Jonathan Hutto, whom I also profiled in *Guys Like Me*, has a deep history of anti-racism activism, both inside and outside the military, including helping to organize the 2013 protest in front of the Department of Justice, following the Trayvon Martin verdict.[11] Three years later, partly in response to Donald Trump's threat of imposing a "Muslim Ban" in the United States, VFP invited Hutto to co-organize their "Veterans Challenge Islamophobia" initiative. He hoped that he could leverage his status as a veteran to "bring a certain legitimized voice to the struggle" and to highlight for the public that "Muslims are veterans and veterans are Muslims." Hutto also intended this work to draw attention to the connections between domestic police violence against African Americans and the nation's "long history of imperialism against darker peoples," most recently in predominantly Muslim nations. By the time *Guys Like Me* was published in 2019, however, Hutto had become frustrated with what he experienced as the glacial movement of VFP's anti-racist organizing efforts. Though he remains aligned with VFP and About Face, he decided his efforts as an organizer would be better utilized in community-based anti-racism organizations.

The diverse cohort of post-9/11 veterans that are the focus of this book bring two important contributions to current mobilizations for racial and economic justice. First, they deliver to social justice coalitions specific knowledge and skills that emanate from their military training. Second, they provide an understanding of the ways that militarization connects with poverty, racism, and colonialism, a perspective that can deepen the critical analysis of movement activists, groups, and coalitions.

Converting military skills to progressive use

When I first interviewed Monique Salhab in 2019, they were working as the interim co-director of the Albuquerque Center for Peace and Justice. It was fulfilling work, Salhab told me, and it allowed them to develop their community organizing skills, including providing training for social justice activists. In September 2019, Donald Trump's campaign announced that the president would visit Albuquerque to rally his supporters. In advance of his visit, the Proud Boys—a group of Trump supporters and violence provocateurs labelled by the Southern Poverty Law Center as a hate group and an "alt-right fight club"—announced they would hold a rally in Albuquerque. Eventually, about 20 Proud Boys and their allies showed up, some clad in helmets and protective gear. They were far outnumbered by community counter-protestors—a coalition of anti-fascist, feminist, LGBTQ2S and immigrant rights activists—chanting "love not hate."[12] Trump showed up for his rally in Albuquerque two days later—at which he was depicted posing with at least one of the Proud Boys—and the community counter-demonstrations swelled.

The counter-protestors didn't just show up out of nowhere to confront the Proud Boys and Donald Trump; their actions were well-planned, their strategies based in part on trainings from Monique Salhab and Salhab's colleagues at the Center for Peace and Justice. The trainings, Salhab told me, involved bringing military experience to bear:

[We were] trying to educate community members about like, "Here's what you'll likely encounter. Here's how they set up perimeters." And trying to teach individuals, folks in the community, to take in some of that strategic-level of planning that folks don't do in the peace movement. You know? Because they look at it, "All that's very militaristic." And it's like, "No, no. You've got to have strategy about what you're going to do if you're going to do an action."

On the day of the encounter with the Proud Boys, Salhab's military knowledge was put to good use for the counter-protestors. In addition to scrutinizing the body language of the Proud Boys, Salhab was carefully watching the police, and also fellow counter-protestors, looking for signs of trouble that might be avoided.

[I]t was a pretty warm day. The police are wearing all this gear. That gear is probably weighing about 30 pounds. They each have one bottle of water, which is not enough. Their patience is going to probably last maybe about an hour and a half. I'm telling the organizers, "Look, you need to come up with a plan about what you want to do next. Because if you don't, they're going to hit their breaking point and they're going to make a decision for us." You know? And so, bringing that level of calculating is helpful because people don't look at that.

While Salhab puts "tactical" skills to use to prevent violence in street demonstrations, Wendy Barranco utilizes her medical skills—honed in the OR in Tikrit, Iraq—in her community organizing. In recent years, Barranco has worked in affiliation with Ground Game LA and People Organized for Westside Renewal, two Los Angeles organizations building grassroots efforts to advance economic and racial justice. Barranco appreciates the broad connections these organizations make—"working in silos is part of the problem"—and she has found that her medical experience is especially useful as part of larger community leadership trainings for newly forming coalitions of women of color, who often have "very little emergency medical experience, and I think that could be dangerous." Barranco also put her background in medical training to use when the COVID-19 pandemic descended on Southern California, hitting poor, immigrant, and communities of color especially hard.

When the pandemic hit, a lot of us already knew each other from movement work, from Ground Game LA. We're all in this same ecosystem. We just organically started coalescing around like, "We need to assess this. We need to do something about this." I started gravitating toward the medic, the decontamination piece, infection control piece. Because there's not really that skill-set in that group. So we developed it from the ground up and it was really touch-and-go. It was really tough. It was really stressful. I found myself jumping into a deployment mode, in the early weeks of this pandemic, of just having to triage and figure that out.

The group's mobilization to set up a community mutual aid system was quick and nimble, "consistently ahead of the state by a week." They raised $150,000, developed a way for people in need to request food or medical support, cleared out the Ground Game LA office and transformed it for food and medical supply storage, and organized a group of trucks and drivers to deliver to needy people throughout LA County. "Jumping into deployment mode," with tactics "extrapolated from my OR experience in the Army," Barranco took charge of ensuring everything was sterile and decontaminated, as she also helped to develop a remote community medical consultation team.

Connecting the dots

In addition to bringing skills to social movement and community actions, veterans often supply a critical analysis of militarism that is too often otherwise missing in progressive coalitions. Stephen Funk conveys this idea in his work with About Face and in his public education efforts.

Militarism is in direct conflict with almost everything, if you're trying to make progress. If you're spending time and energy funding war, you're not funding education and healthcare. Militarism makes cops be able to do whatever they want, because this idea that the military, the protectors, the people with guns are above it all, and they can get away with everything, is not something that has to be. It just is how we are doing it, and the people in the communities that are hurting the most understand that. And they can make that connection.

Similarly, Monique Salhab deepens conversations in anti-racism groups by "connecting the dots" between police brutality against people of color with militarization and wars. "The terrorism overseas that the military brings to other countries," Salhab says, is related to "the terror that people of color face in their own communities here in the United States by law enforcement, which receives equipment from the military surplus program." Indeed, sociologist Tom Nolan's research shows how police militarization, which "began in earnest in the aftermath of the terrorist attacks on Sept. 11, 2001," has involved the transfer of "military-grade equipment" to police forces, and training that leads police to see protestors not as citizens, but as "the enemy." This "militarized police mentality," Nolan argues, "can be deadly, especially for Black Americans."[13] Monique Salhab has realized that part of their job involves bringing that knowledge to anti-racism community activists.

In all of the work that I do, I am always bringing in that vantage point, connecting the dots so that people actually see how the military is the root cause of everything going on in our society, whether it's jobs, healthcare, the environment. And sometimes it's very difficult because there are folks who are just like, "Well, the military doesn't have anything to do with White privilege." And I'm just like, "Oh, no, it does." I am a big believer that if there were a deconstruction of the military, that the elements of patriarchy, White fragility and White supremacy culture behaviors, and queer phobia and all of the things that intersect with that would start to crumble.

These individual efforts by Funk and Salhab to bring a critique of militarization to community coalitions reflects larger organizational efforts, including About Face's "Drop the MIC" campaign, as well as a spring 2020 webinar series on militarization, psychological warfare, and colonialism, presented by Monisha Ríos, along with Jovanni Reyes and other About Face members.

Neither the military-based skills nor the anti-militarism perspective that VFP and About Face activists bring to economic and racial justice coalitions are always accepted with open arms. Phoenix Johnson is wary of the shallow "recreational activism within the White demographic" in the Seattle-area coalitions they are connected with. Johnson worries about their small About Face group's activism being dissipated or wasted as they risk "putting ourselves into a vacuum of problematic White activism that's exclusionary." And at times it has been a struggle for Johnson to convince fellow VFP chapter members that anti-racist coalition work is relevant. When "the only Black veteran" in Johnson's chapter proposed forming a partnership with the local MLK Coalition, a White member "threw a wet blanket" on the idea, balking at an $80 fee, and expressing a concern that "Well, we haven't evaluated if their organization aligns with our values." Exasperated, Johnson replied, ""What do you mean, *if they align with our values?*" I was like, "They *absolutely* align with our values!"

Wendy Barranco faced some push-back from another direction. When she was charged with doing some medic training for a group of young women of color community activists, she was enthused to share the knowledge she had amassed from her military combat experience. When she emphasized to the group that they sorely needed more "general medical resiliency training in the community to continue to take care of ourselves and the community," the message was not well received. Several women in the group rejected Barranco's military-based knowledge, arguing that "it comes from a colonizer imperialist system, right? A colonized medical perspective." Barranco did not disagree entirely with their criticism, acknowledging that it made her think more deeply that "I do have work left to do to decolonize my thinking." Still, she continues to believe of her military medical experience, "there's pragmatic skills value there" that social movement groups too often lack.

a taste of her own medicine

Sexual and gender justice

About Face and VFP coalition work with racial and economic justice groups has proceeded at close to full throttle in recent years. Meanwhile, the organizations' efforts to couple with recent efforts to address feminist and LGBTQ2S concerns have mostly sputtered. On the surface, the groups' limited action on gender and sexual issues may seem odd, especially given the veterans' stories in Chapter 2 that recount a steady drum-beat of gender and sexual violation and humiliation suffered by women and queer military service members. These collective experiences, as Brittany DeBarros told me, fuel a sense of urgency among her cohort of emergent leaders, to build connections between their anti-war work with "the liberation and claiming of our bodies, to anti-patriarchal work: thinking of war and the military as this institution that degrades your own value of your body, and asks you to hate your body in the process of hurting other bodies, and just the way that those are so connected with sexuality and sexual oppression."

Nevertheless, as Monisha Ríos told me, her efforts in VFP—including organizing a workshop on rape culture with Monique Salhab at a national VFP convention—revealed the membership's interest in these issues as "pretty stagnant—I see the evidence of it in the unwillingness of the people to even have a conversation about rape as warfare." Even About Face—a younger organization, with more women of color among its leadership—is "way behind" the national conversation on gender-based violence, according to Wendy Barranco. "It's not as bad as VFP, but I think over time, as long as I've been with About Face, to be honest with you, [they] haven't really tackled those questions of gender and sexuality. They're way, way, way, behind."

How do we explain the relative dearth of VFP and About Face organizing to address gender and sexuality issues, especially during a time of resurgent feminist activism concerning gender-based violence, sexual harassment, and pay equity in workplaces? For one thing, the emergent women of color and queer leadership in veterans' peace organizations find themselves in an historically familiar position with respect to race and gender politics. They are, to draw from a concept introduced by sociologist Patricia Hill Collins, "outsiders-within," a status in which a "creative tension" inheres: they are women *of color* within a White-dominated feminist movement; they are *women* within racial justice and veterans' peace movements that, until recently, have been male-dominated.[14] Historically, women of color have drawn from their intersectional knowledge to play a bridging role in social movements: "bringing" sexuality and gender issues to racial justice movements, and pressing race (and often also social class) to the center of feminist analysis and action.

Being responsible for doing this bridge work can be frustrating and exhausting; more than once while I conducted the research for this book, the title of Cherríe Moraga and Gloria Anzaldua's foundational 1981 women of color anthology came to mind: *This Bridge Called My Back*.[15] There is a long history of women of color who take on the burden of *being* bridges across communities being punished, on the one hand, as "divisive" by men leaders in racial justice movements for raising gender issues and, on the other hand, ignored and marginalized in women's movements when they pushed for serious engagements with racism.[16] Reflecting this broader pattern, the emergent women of color and queer leaders in About Face and VFP have at times been frustrated when they raise "women's issues" like military sexual trauma, which some older members view as "divisive" issues that divert veterans' peace organizations from their central "mission." And as a "Two-Spirit and gender nonconforming" Native person, Phoenix Johnson deals with similar outsider-within frustrations in attempting to bridge VFP with Indigenous organizations. In VFP circles, some members still do not know what Two-Spirit people are. And Johnson found Native Two-Spirit communities in both Portland and Seattle to be very unaccepting of her bodily self-presentation.

> I was too femme, too woman, and they're misogynist. That's how colonized we are. If you're gay and bi, the Two-Spirit world rolls out the rainbow carpet for you. But someone like me, people are very confused by me because they look at my body and hypersexualize my body and then see me as a femme person, so then they treat me like a woman versus like a Two-Spirit person. So I can never get away from some of the bullshit.

Some women of color activists I spoke with also expressed reluctance to get involved in feminist movement efforts—for instance the annual anti-Trump "Women's March"—that they see as having been shaped and driven by "White feminists" who have ignored, excluded or marginalized women of color in the movement.

Several veterans expressed to me their impatience with their organizations' lack of movement on sexuality and gender issues, and their determination to press these issues closer to the center of internal discussions and coalitional efforts. Meanwhile, some individuals have initiated efforts to build community coalitions around gender and sexuality issues. Stephen Funk, for instance, was the creative director of Veteran Artists, a San Francisco Bay Area theatre effort that had a successful ten-year run. The group's most successful stage effort ran between 2009–2012, bringing together local veterans and drag queens for "Make Drag, Not War," performing stories written by veterans of the Afghanistan and Iraq wars, addressing veterans' issues like PTSD and Don't Ask, Don't Tell.[17]

Monisha Ríos, for a time, engaged with an effort to reform how the VA deals with military sexual trauma, especially for women veterans. She had concluded from her own experience with the VA that "It's not designed for us. Going to the VA at all was a gauntlet, for a lot of us. Some women don't have this experience,

I am glad, but most of us do. It's still the harassment, groping, attempted assault, and then it's swept under the rug by the professionals who work in the building." Ríos found a group called "Service: When women come marching home"[18] that made her feel like she finally "had a platform and a voice."

> I started going to rallies, and getting invited to go testify at Congress, and talking with reporters, and you know, I became somewhat of a leader within the movement. I started a group called "Leave No One Behind." My goal was to create this, where it was led by veterans, where it was informed by MST survivors, and where we create a curriculum. This was my big goal. It did not materialize. 'Cause I couldn't do it. I was still suffering a lot.

Despite the false start of Leave No One Behind, Ríos remained determined to address women veterans' issues. "Look at how many women veterans are homeless. We're not counted properly. We're not even acknowledged most of the time. Our needs are not considered still." But she knew she could not tackle this issue alone and was convinced that the work needed to be rooted in a progressive veterans' organization. When she was invited to serve on the VFP board, she was hopeful that the organization would give her a platform for addressing MST and other gender issues, but she eventually concluded that VFP's commitment to gender issues "was like lip service." She left her board position in frustration.

Brittany DeBarros's recent ascendance to leadership in About Face, however, has some people feeling hopeful that gender and sexuality issues might gain some traction in that organization. As Wendy Barranco told me, "Since Brittany got hired, About Face has grown leaps and bounds. Leaps and bounds. That's all really to her credit, because she's pushing the organization to where I think it needs to be. And I think her power comes from her vision, but also that she's been an officer in the military." Stephen Funk echoed this optimistic view of About Face: "I think it's great that it's mostly female leadership, and it's coming from that place that will no longer tolerate that type of environment that we had come from before."

White Saviors, or decolonization accomplices?

In the spring of 2016, tribal members from the Standing Rock Sioux Reservation in North Dakota sparked a grassroots movement to block the building of the Dakota Access Pipeline, an 1172-mile-long oil conduit that, among other things, would run below the Missouri and Mississippi Rivers, threatening the health, safety, and sovereignty of Native lands and peoples. Calling themselves "Water Protectors," the opposition movement grew by September into a massive coalition of Native tribes and their allies, demanding Indigenous sovereignty over their lands. Conflicts ensued: In October, riot-gear-clad police and their dogs violently cleared an encampment of Water Protectors; in freezing November temperatures, police blasted protestors with water cannons. It was then that a coalition of U.S. military veterans announced they would go to Standing Rock to serve as "human shields" for the Water Protectors against the militarized police violence waged in support of Big Oil.

Eventually as many as 4,000 veterans, including members of VFP and About Face, arrived in Standing Rock during the depths of a freezing winter.[19] The veterans' presence at Standing Rock amplified the visibility of the Water Protectors' cause in the national media, and by early December there was a moment of optimism as the Obama administration paused the building of the pipeline for an assessment of the project's environmental impact. The veterans' time at Standing Rock was punctuated by a powerful December 4 "forgiveness ceremony," wherein two leaders of their delegation—army veteran Wesley Clark, Jr. (son of retired Army General Wesley Clark, Sr.), and marine corps veteran Michael A. Wood, Jr., knelt before tribal elders Arvol Looking Horse, Faith Spotted Eagle, Phyllis Young, Paula Horne, Jon Eagle, Sr., and Leonard Crow Dog, as Clark said the following words:

> Many of us, me particularly, are from the units that have hurt you over the many years. We came. We fought you. We took your land. We signed treaties that we broke. We stole minerals from your sacred hills. We blasted the faces of our presidents onto your sacred mountain. Then we took still more land and then we took your children and . . . we tried to eliminate your language that God gave you, and the Creator gave you. We didn't respect you, we polluted your Earth, we've hurt you in so many ways but we've come to say that we are sorry. We are at your service and we beg for your forgiveness.[20]

The Water Protectors' victory over Big Oil, the federal government, and its militarized police was short-lived. By early 2017, newly inaugurated President Donald Trump scrapped Obama-era environmental protection studies and decreed that the pipeline would proceed. In February, the National Guard forcibly removed the remaining protestors, and the pipeline was completed by May. But the Water Protectors had inspired Indigenous Peoples around the nation and the world, galvanizing and deepening connections between environmental activism and Indigenous decolonization movements. And the veterans who joined the struggle had shown how former members of the U.S. military could engage in ritual acts of reconciliation for their complicity in historic acts of land theft and genocide, and how they could put their bodies on the line to support struggles by Indigenous peoples.

Phoenix Johnson's experience reveals the complicated realities of veterans' actions at Standing Rock. In November of 2016, "I watched on TV and I was horrified, and I watched them get sprayed with the water in the middle of the night in below freezing temperatures." Not long thereafter, when the call went out for veterans to go to Standing Rock, Johnson was ready to dive in, and as a Native Two-Spirit VFP member Johnson assumed this would be "my first big organizing undertaking." Johnson immediately started to coordinate Portland-area About Face and VFP members for the trip to Standing Rock. When Johnson noted that among the national leadership of the veterans' Standing Rock effort, "almost none of us are Indigenous," Johnson told the veterans' coalition, "I'm going to propose that we have an Indigenous, non-Indigenous organizing pair in each state that is going. We'll have that cultural competency and we're building our strategy in an effective way and centering what's important. And they basically told me to fuck off." Johnson was unceremoniously kicked off the organizing team. "So, 72 hours ahead of time I had to tell my veterans I'm sorry. I can't lead you."

Undaunted, Phoenix Johnson drove to Standing Rock on their own, and experienced the days there as "very intense." Johnson was alarmed with how—despite the fact that Clark's and Wood's umbrella organization, *Veterans' Stand*, had quickly raised $1.4 million to support veterans at Standing Rock—many of the freshly arrived veterans were receiving no support services.[21] As someone who had recently been doing suicide prevention work with veterans, Johnson worried about the veterans' well-being.

> It was an unsafe environment for them. It was 40 below, dead of winter, ten feet of snow, I swear. It was underequipped. They were not getting resources that they were promised. When we're organizing we have to effectively strategize around a population that is heavily laden with certain disabilities and other challenges. They didn't want to hear me and I said we're going to

have veterans blowing out. And sure enough, one of mine, too, had a complete mental breakdown and was found without any shoes, jacket, nothing, walking through the snow.

I told Johnson that I had watched video of Wesley Clark and Michael Wood's reconciliation ceremony with tribal elders, and had found it very moving. Johnson agreed that it was moving but was doubtful of its lasting effect. "I think those demonstrations need to be seen and they need to be done around the country, and it also needs to be followed—preceded and followed—with authentic relationship-building and reconciliation." I asked Johnson if they think that sort of lasting and "authentic relationship-building" between veterans and Indigenous people happened following Standing Rock.

> No. Mike Woods and Wesley Clark are awful . . . and because of all of the shit that I faced in the organizing team, I was ready to chew Mike Woods's face off. I got that moment. He was just a sitting duck. I walked right up to him and let him have it. I just called out all of the issues that we were having: that they were not effectively collaborating with Indigenous people, that this was just another expression of White supremacy and White saviorism. They were just here to benefit themselves. To make themselves look good.

Despite their blistering criticism of the leadership team, Johnson did observe that "There were veterans in the space that actually cared. There were veterans who were being activated for the first time in their lives and I got to witness that." One of these vets told Johnson, " 'I don't know how or why I'm out here, but I'm crying and I feel like I'm becoming a part of something important.' And I'm like, 'You are, and here's how you can continue to do that.' I mean, they were rubbing their eyes and blinking like they were just waking up."

Phoenix Johnson's story reveals the deep fissures that lie just below the surface of the widely circulated story of veterans as supportive allies in the struggles of Indigenous Peoples at Standing Rock. One tension lies in the common cultural assumption that military veterans (often culturally coded as White Americans) and Indigenous Peoples (coded as racialized Others) are viewed as two, discrete groups. For instance, U.S. troops' tendency to talk about enemy-controlled territory in Iraq or Afghanistan as "Indian Country," according to anthropologist Stephen Silliman, is a metaphor that "represents the language of colonization in the present."[22] Native leader Winona LaDuke makes a less metaphorical point in her book, *The Militarization of Indian Country*: "At the beginning of the twenty-first century, there are between 160,000 and 190,000 Native American military veterans, about 10% of all living Native Americans. This is a proportion triple to that of the non-Indian population. An estimated 22% of Native Americans 18 or older are veterans."[23] This Native-veteran overlap was rendered largely invisible at Standing Rock, in part due to the exclusionary dynamics that Phoenix Johnson experienced in the formation of the veterans' leadership team, and also due to the visible positioning of White male veterans like Clark and Woods.

Phoenix Johnson and others have raised a more fundamental question: What did the presence of up to 4,000 veterans contribute to the effort at Standing Rock? A Native activist interviewed by *Vice News* noted that the veterans "brought cameras," increasing the struggle's media visibility, but otherwise saw the poorly organized veterans' effort as "a real shit show . . . It seemed as if they focused on pictures and [media] stories instead of having accountability of all personnel."[24] The veterans' action at Standing Rock highlights a common question in social movement coalitions: how can predominantly White groups (or those with visible White leadership) serve as supportive allies in racial justice or decolonial movements? The "colonial trope of the White savior," in the words of sociologist Jeffrey Montez de Oca, so evident in popular film and the mass media, positions oppressed peoples as needing salvation from generous, patronizing White people.[25] In social movement contexts like at Standing Rock, the White Savior Complex positions White leaders (and often, as in this case, White *men* leaders) squarely in front of the TV cameras. As they step into the public spotlight, White Saviors risk rendering invisible the very people who have provided the leadership and grassroots organizing that has created the movement. In so doing—even if they are simply parachuting in for a few days, before leaving—they may also create the impression that they are the leaders of struggles that were in fact started and developed by Indigenous Peoples and other people of color. In what might be the definitive book-length examination of the Standing Rock opposition to the Dakota Access Pipeline, Indigenous scholar Nick Estes devotes but two sentences to the veterans' appearance at Standing Rock, perhaps underlining the outsized media splash their abbreviated stint received during a much deeper and protracted struggle that was disproportionately led, Estes argues, by Indigenous women and Two-Spirit people.[26]

Veterans For Peace has a long history of sponsoring international delegations in support of liberation or anti-militarism struggles of local peoples in Central America, Palestine, Okinawa, and elsewhere. In recent years, some younger VFP members have criticized what they see as the "colonizing" and "White Savior" modes that those delegations have taken. Monisha Ríos was invited to join a VFP delegation to Okinawa, in support of a longstanding movement by local activists to stop the expansion of U.S. military bases on the Japanese island.[27] Ríos gladly went along. She was impressed with the local activists, but was appalled with some of her fellow VFP delegates.

> It's again a situation where the White dudes are running the show. And they're the favorites in VFP. They're the ones everyone thinks is great and like, they're heroes. But meanwhile, they're over there co-opting a 70-plus-year movement of people who survived the battle in Okinawa. Who are trying to protect their own people, who are Indigenous people, too, who want actual fucking help and allyship and solidarity, but what they get is, you know, a bunch of glory-seeking photo-opping folks, who also make it colonial, because they're there imposing their way of doing things on these people.

Vic, an older White VFP member who has joined a number of international VFP delegations, takes issue with Ríos's criticism.

> It's very explicit wherever we go that we are there at the request of the local activists and we are to follow the local activists' lead. And we do what they ask us to do. Whether it's in Palestine or Okinawa or Standing Rock, that is made very clear at the outset. And generally they ask us to be out front because it's more valuable to them to say, "Hey, U.S. oppressors or U.S.-supported oppressors, here's some U.S. vets." So it's *at the request* of the Okinawan chapter of Veterans For Peace or various Palestinian activists that we've worked with: They will tend to position us right in the front, which may create a misimpression that here are the Great White Saviors or something. But every delegation I've been on, that's been very clear from the outset. We are here to do what they ask us to do. It can be viewed as "here's the White Saviors positioning themselves in the media," but it doesn't get into the media unless you are out there out front.

Vic's description underlines a built-in contradiction in veterans' ally efforts, especially so long as the veterans who are "out there out front" in the media spotlight are exclusively or mostly White men: Their very presence tends to draw much-needed media attention to the struggle; at the same time, the "optics" of White men out in front reinforces their cultural centrality, while further marginalizing the colonized people of color who are actually at the heart of the movement. Brittany DeBarros has a nuanced view of the public optics of this built-in contradiction. "It's not malicious," she said, but "when you're showing up in solidarity, it's not a great look to show up with a thousand VFP flags and hats and stuff. Because it's kind of making yourself the center of attention in a way that's really frustrating for folks, just lacks self-awareness." In contrast, DeBarros thinks About Face's younger and more diverse post-9/11 veterans are striving to be more sensitive in how they support "decolonization struggles" generated by communities that have suffered harm from U.S. militarism, colonialism, and racism:

> We as people who fought in this generation's wars, I think have a deeper sensitivity to that because we are closer to it, right? We understand. Like, I'm never going to blame Iraqi people for being skeptical of me, you know. And my role in being in solidarity with them, [I] do whatever the fuck they tell me that is helpful to them. Right. And that's it, period. If I'm showing up for them, let's not make it about vets, unless they want it to be about vets, to like give them cover.

The fine line that veterans navigate between positioning themselves either as colonial White Saviors or as supportive allies is especially narrow, often perilously so, when they attempt to support efforts driven by Indigenous Peoples. Sociologist Corrie Grosse emphasizes that it is important to see the mobilization at Standing Rock not simply as a part of the environmental movement. Instead, "at its center [it was] part of a long legacy of Indigenous organizing for sovereignty and decolonization." [28] And as Eve Tuck and K. Wayne Yang have argued, "Decolonization, which we assert is a distinct project from other civil and human rights-based social justice projects, is far too often subsumed into the directives of these projects, with no regard for how decolonization wants something different than those forms of justice." [29] At its core, the "something different" that Indigenous projects seek involves revealing, resisting, and reversing how historical projects of White settler colonialism supplanted Indigenous knowledge systems, and returning

Indigenous sovereignty over stolen lands. This suggests that VFP or About Face's efforts to engage in coalition work with Indigenous Peoples' decolonization efforts face qualitatively different challenges than their intersectional coalition work with other social justice projects, such as Black Lives Matter or movements to end gender-based violence. Put another way, decolonization efforts introduce knowledge and goals that are not always obviously in sync with conventional intersectional (race, class, gender, sexuality) social justice movements.

"Stop the War on Mother Earth"

At their 2019 national convention, Veterans For Peace overwhelmingly passed a resolution, introduced by Korean War veteran and longtime VFP member Woody Powell, calling on local VFP chapters to join with organizations that are working to arrest climate change, and to engage in educational work to raise awareness of the links between militarism and environmental destruction.[30] The VFP resolution came in the wake of a rapidly expanding global youth movement, sparked in 2018 by Swedish teen Greta Thunberg, demanding action to arrest climate change. Massive public demonstrations and "Fridays for Future" school "climate strikes" by students stretched through 2019. The United Nations held a 2019 "Climate Action Summit" and various national governments pressed for action to address what was increasingly being framed as a global climate emergency.

As much of the international community took steps toward reducing carbon emissions, the U.S. government was moving in the opposite direction. President Donald Trump pulled the U.S. endorsement of the 2015 Paris Climate Accord, while moving to reverse domestic fuel emission standards and eliminate environmental regulations on coal and fracking. After the November 2018 "blue wave" election gave Democrats control of Congress, and echoing the demands of youth climate activists in the "Sunrise Movement," Representative Alexandria Ocasio-Cortez and Senator Ed Markey proposed a "Green New Deal." The legislation had no chance of being passed in the Republican-controlled Senate, much less being signed by President Trump. But the Green New Deal became a rallying-call for progressives seeking national action to redirect resources toward the dual goal of building a "green" economy that drastically reduced carbon emissions while also creating good jobs.

As the Green New Deal was being introduced in Congress, the women's peace organization CODEPINK appealed to Representative Ocasio-Cortez and Senator Markey that any such national effort, to be successful, needed simultaneously to address the ways that militarization was intertwined with environmental destruction. In a summary statement, CODEPINK's Medea Benjamin observed that "The U.S. military is the single largest consumer of fossil fuels in the world," spewing huge volumes of carbon into the air annually; recent U.S. wars in the Middle East were "fought to protect the interests of Big Oil"; U.S. military operations around the world "leave a toxic legacy in their wake," and U.S. wars "ravage fragile ecosystems." The bloated Pentagon budget, Benjamin added, "monopolizes the funding we need to seriously address the climate crisis."[31]

In its 2019 resolution, VFP echoed many of these points and argued that local chapters needed to contribute an understanding of militarism and war as major sources of climate change to the burgeoning climate action movement. The San Diego, California, chapter of VFP created a website that illuminated these links and provided information and resources for addressing climate change.[32] The Santa Fe, New Mexico, VFP chapter that I am affiliated with partnered as a supporter of Youth United for Climate Crisis Action.[33] When YUCCA organized several thousand people to march on the New Mexico State Roundhouse (Capitol building) on September 20, 2019, to protest climate change, I joined a dozen or so VFP members who marched amidst a sea of young people behind a large "Stop the War on Mother Earth" banner (Figure 4.3). In subsequent weeks, smaller numbers of VFP members joined groups of young protestors during their Friday "climate strikes" at the Roundhouse. On one such occasion, I stood with three VFP members sporting VFP banners as young people repeatedly phoned the governor's office, urging her to declare a climate emergency. One of the VFP members present told me that he was excited by the upsurge of youth activism, and while he hoped that VFP could contribute information about militarization and war to the burgeoning movement, "we just want to be in the background, not step on their plate, you know? They want to do their own thing."

By the end of 2019, veterans were making moves toward allying with climate change activists on several fronts. Longtime VFP member Vic echoed the growing consensus in VFP that climate change "is the issue of our times. Unless we address militarism, the species is doomed. It's not the elephant in the room; it's the herd of elephants in the room." About Face member Wendy Barranco echoed this sentiment: "It's tied, right? If we're trying to tackle the

Figure 4.3 Veterans For Peace members join youth-led "Climate Strike," Santa Fe, NM, September 20, 2019
Photo by author

climate crisis, then we also need to be talking about the Military Industrial Complex. And that's the piece that has been absent from a lot of the narrative out there, right? The environmental organizations, for the most part, don't say a thing about it." As VFP and About Face pivoted to contribute to the surge of climate activism in the United States and the world, other intersectional issues were raised as well. Another VFP member, Santiago, agreed with others' points about the need to address militarism, but—and echoing the advocates of the Green New Deal—he also emphasized that the ways climate change is tackled must be grounded in environmental justice. "Climate change and poverty," he emphasized, "fundamentally, what else is there to work on?"

In New Mexico and other areas of the Southwest, Indigenous groups provide an answer to Santiago's question. A Green New Deal is not enough, argued The Red Nation, a Native liberation organization.[34] Infusing climate change activism with a decolonial logic, they argue, will transform a Green New Deal into a "Red Deal."[35] Past energy technologies, especially when coupled with war-making—think oil pipelines, fracking, uranium mining, nuclear bomb development and testing, and storage of nuclear waste— have disproportionately devastated Indigenous lands and people. The Red Nation asserts that any efforts to develop a "green" economy—for instance, the building of massive wind and solar farms—must not further expropriate, exploit, or destroy Native lands and people; rather, such policies should be explicitly "red," constructed to empower Indigenous peoples, enhance their health, and restore their sovereignty over their lands.

As a local social justice activist in Albuquerque, New Mexico, Monique Salhab began to learn about decolonization from The Red Nation, Pueblo Action Alliance, and other Indigenous organizations. "I started thinking about it in relation to our work within VFP. And I thought, well, we don't talk about this, we don't talk about decolonizing. We talk about, yes, being war resistors, having fought in the military. But there is a connection to that and decolonization that is huge." Salhab is impressed with how decolonial movements "connect the dots" in ways that others often do not: "The Red Nation centered military divestment in the Red Deal. Whereas The Green New Deal mentions it, it's there a little bit, but it's not centered."

When Native leader and writer Winona LaDuke connects these dots, it becomes apparent how Indigenous Peoples across the globe are in a deadly web spun by U.S. militarism and colonial war-making: "In all cases, Indigenous people of the Americas are linked to the Hiroshima and Nagasaki bombs, as well as to the more than a thousand nuclear tests under-taken in the Pacific and Nevada."[36] The 2020 VFP national convention in Albuquerque, New Mexico, was planned to correspond with a broad coa-lition of peace activists who would descend upon nearby Los Alamos, the cradle that birthed the bombs that the United States dropped on Hiroshima and Nagasaki, 75 years ago.[37] The convention planners intended to create a program that included the voices of Japanese people, and also Native peoples of the Southwest who are disproportionately among the uranium miners[38] and the "Downwinders" who have suffered escalated cancer deaths and other health problems due to radioactive exposure from atomic bomb tests in the 1950s and 1960s.[39]

What was expected to be a massive turnout in Los Alamos for a somber remembrance of the U.S. bombings of Hiroshima and Nagasaki, and a pro-test of continuing nuclear weapons production and militarization, was short-circuited by the COVID-19 pandemic, as VFP shifted gears for an online national convention that retained its focus on preventing nuclear war and promoting a broad demilitarization of society and the world. Meanwhile, in the spring and summer of 2020, organizations ranging from VFP and About Face to Red Nation and YUCCA pivoted into public activism in support of the national uprising for racial justice, as they also contributed to coalitions seeking to provide mutual aid for COVID-19 health and economic struggles facing already-precarious poor, of color, and Indigenous populations.

***

This chapter illustrates how members of VFP and About Face deal with "the extension dilemma," the common quandary that social movement organizations face in strategizing how much to remain tightly focused on their organization's defined "mission"—in this case, opposing militarism and promoting peace—versus extending organization resources and effort to engage in coalitions with progressive organizations working on a wide range of social justice or decolonization efforts. I have shown that the ways that VFP and About Face navigate the extension dilemma is a matter of some internal debate and disagreement. These differences are apparent across generational cohorts of activists, but they are by no means categorical; rather, they are a matter of degree or relative emphasis.

Sometimes criticized by younger activists for narrowly focusing their activism on war and peace, the older cohort of VFP members has long engaged in coalition work, both domestically and internationally. However, the membership's situated knowledge—generally grounded in their experiences as older White, heterosexual men—has translated into a collective praxis that leans toward remaining focused on "the mission" of VFP, while connecting with other social justice efforts in one of two ways. First, as many of their recent actions with the youth-led climate change movement illustrates, VFP members frequently "show up" with their VFP signs and banners, in visible but somewhat passive support of others' efforts. Or second, as with some of their "delegations" (such as to Okinawa, Palestine, or Standing Rock), VFP members place themselves visibly "out in front" of local movement groups, with the goal of expanding media attention to the group's cause.

Either strategy has built-in benefits as well as limitations and strains. The first—showing up with banners in passive support—helps to build a public presence for VFP as a supportive element in broad community coalitions. But to the extent that members mostly just show up with their VFP banners, they limit the ways that they can contribute to deepening the work of coalitions; for instance, despite showing up in support of myriad climate change protests, VFP has not yet developed mechanisms through which it might contribute a much-needed analysis of the central importance of militarism in climate change activism. On the other hand, when veterans position themselves "out in front" of other social movements—even when invited to do so by local activists in order to expand media attention for their cause—they risk being viewed as "White Saviors" who are appropriating the media limelight and claiming organizational leadership. The dangers of this public positioning as "White Saviors" are most dire when the veterans are all or mostly White men, positioned "out in front" in support of social justice efforts by people of color or anti-colonial struggles by Indigenous people.

The younger cohort of veterans that I have focused on here—members of VFP and/or About Face—share a collective knowledge situated in being veterans, but also in being people of color, women, gender non-binary and/or queer. This intersectional-knowledge standpoint fuels a general tendency among progressive millennials to take a skeptical view of "siloed" organizations that work mostly on single issues; instead, this younger cohort of activists leans into a collective praxis of intersectional coalition politics. This tendency too has its strengths and its potential pitfalls. The main promise of the younger cohort's intersectional praxis lies in its ability to understand connections (both analytically and viscerally, from experience): militarism and war are linked with racial injustice, colonialism, gender and sexual violence, and environmental destruction. From this organic understanding of intersectional connections springs a collective commitment to build a transformative movement, as activists bridge those connections, nimbly and flexibly shifting their loci of activism to issues that become salient in the historical moment.

There are strains built into the intersectional coalition politics of the ascendant cohort of activists, not the least of which is the potential burnout that individual activists face, especially women of color tasked with serving as "bridges" across and between different organizations. A second strain concerns the very future of VFP and About Face as organizations. In the final chapter, I will continue to center on the stories of the younger cohort of veterans to consider the promise and risks facing VFP: Will it grow and change, or will it ossify within a hardened silo and gradually fade in importance as its older membership ages out? About Face, I will suggest, encounters a different range of promise and risk: Will the organization

grow its niche in the larger social movement ecology, contributing a crucially important critique of militarism and war? Or, might About Face's
identity and organizational structure eventually dissipate as its members
melt through its permeable boundaries into intersectional action in the
larger ecology of movement activism?

Interlude 4
"Say it, mean it, and do something about it"

On August 2, 2020, I joined about 425 people who attended the Veterans For Peace annual national convention, held online due to the COVID-19 epidemic. Garett Reppenhagen, the VFP executive director, invited Yaqui Nation member Eli Painted Crow, a veteran of 22 years in the U.S. Army, including stints in Iraq and Kuwait, to introduce the opening plenary by delivering a land acknowledgement statement. Short speeches that acknowledge the historical stewardship and continuing relationship of Indigenous Peoples to the specific geographic area on which a meeting is taking place, land acknowledgement statements have in recent years become ritualized ways to begin public events, especially for progressive organizations. In this case, Reppenhagen acknowledged that an online convention meant that participants had their feet planted in many geographic locations, making a land recognition statement perhaps a bit more challenging to deliver. He introduced Eli Painted Crow as "a former member of VFP" and turned the virtual floor over to her.

A long-time peace activist, a voice against sexual assault of women in the military, and co-founder of the Indigenous women's drumming group Turtle Women Rising, Eli Painted Crow had indeed been a VFP member several years ago, including having delivered an address to the national VFP convention in 2006. On this day in 2020, she began her talk by alluding to that connection, before launching into her land recognition statement.

I was really grateful to have this opportunity to participate in this because my experience with Veterans For Peace was quite some time ago, and I've been waiting—I've been waiting for you guys to rise up, you know. I have a really big concern: I was asked to do a land recognition, and I think this is a global kind of thing, that there's probably a lot of Indigenous land that's been taken all over the world, so I found that challenging. The other piece that I found challenging is why people are doing land recognition. I get that it's a way to honor the land and the people who once lived there, but you also need to think about what it does. The best example that I could give is that if I had a car, and one of you took it—one of you non-Native people took it—and told everybody on my block that that was my car, that you acknowledged that it was my car, and then you got in drove off with it. That's what it feels like when I hear "land recognition." It's like, you're telling me something, but are you putting salt in the wound by saying that? Because if you're not doing anything but recognizing the land, that's sort of like when someone comes up to you and says "Thank you for your service," and they're just a bunch of words that don't really mean a whole lot.

So my invitation to all of you who feel that this is important is that I think that every single one of you should know where you live, whose land it was, and I think every single one of you should consider doing [something] to support the people of that nation, as a way of really saying, "I'm recognizing this land, I'm recognizing the people by supporting them in whatever it is they're needing or trying to grow for themselves." Don't just say it to say it. Say it, mean it, and do something about it. Otherwise, they're just empty words and frankly Native people are pretty tired of that kind of stuff.

As I listened, Eli Painted Crow's words sharpened my understanding of the ways that Indigenous decolonization struggles are in some ways congruent with progressive social justice activism, but in other ways they are distinct. Indigenous activists are wary, for good reasons, of their centuries-long struggles for recognition and self-determination being subsumed within larger progressive coalitions, and reduced to symbolic gestures that render Native Peoples as caricatures of the past, rather than as visible living people. I certainly recognized these tensions in the stories I heard about the contradictory meanings and mixed impact of veterans' attempts to serve as allies with Indigenous Water Protectors at Standing Rock in the winter of 2016.

Eli Painted Crow, in this short speech, did not state why she had left VFP years ago, but as she finished her talk, she alluded to both the tensions and to the potential congruences between Indigenous decolonial activism and veterans' anti-militarism. "What does peace mean for this group?" She asked. "Does it just mean absence of war, and trying to stop wars for the past 20 years or so?" She replied to her own questions with an assertion with which I am confident many VFP people agree: "Peace is more than just absence of war; it's a way to live." Over the next few days, as I attended VFP convention sessions on racial justice, nuclear war, and climate change, it was evident to me how some of the non-Indigenous VFP members were consciously stretching to listen to and understand Indigenous peoples' experiences.

5

"You've got to do something radical"

Intersectional praxis in social movements

About Face leader Brittany Ramos DeBarros stood before an audience of Veterans For Peace members and delivered a cross-generational analysis of where the veterans' movement for peace and justice has been, and where it might go. Scarcely two years into the movement, DeBarros acknowledged that she was still a newcomer compared with many in the audience who had worked with VFP for decades, and she then shifted gears to offer a fresh analysis.[1]

> The fact that so many of you have been in this struggle for decades gives me hope. Thank you for creating the space, for holding the space, through decades of invisibility, of uphill battles . . . Sometimes, we go through periods as movements where that's what we need to do—we need to keep the flame alive and hold the space. I feel a visceral conviction that that is not the moment that we are in now. Our work right now is not to hold the space. Our work right now is to move into a new era of opportunity that we have been presented with.

DeBarros's conviction—and her optimism—were grounded in the multiple projects with which she was currently engaged, including her migrant justice action with Wendy Barranco at the U.S.–Mexico border. She noted that it was "exhausting" and perhaps not that effective, for an organization to spend its energies, year after year, in protesting this war, that war, and the next war. While she respected the need for VFP to continue with that work, she proposed a broader agenda.

> I think that it's time for us to come to a unified system-level conversation so that there is a cornerstone of vocabulary that people have. And my theory is based in what has already happened with MeToo, with Black Lives Matter, with Occupy—all of those movements contributed and popularized what

Unconventional Combat. Michael A. Messner, Oxford University Press. © Oxford University Press 2021.
DOI: 10.1093/oso/9780197573631.003.0005

previously had been academic vocabulary . . . We [now] have unprecedented movement momentum in an unprecedently intersectional way.

When I witnessed that speech in the summer of 2019, I was impressed
with DeBarros's analysis, especially her recognition of the ways that
intersectionality was becoming a connective language in a broad
ecology of social movement organizations. I confess, though, that I saw
her optimism as a stretch. Her claim that the movement faced "a new
era of opportunity" and that there was currently "unprecedented movement momentum" seemed a bit to me like a young leader trying to in-
fuse hope in her tiring charges for one more up-hill push. I had come to
view VFP and About Face as impressive organizations doing crucially
important work, but also as small and possibly shrinking groups, with
core members working hard to "hold space," engaging in what social
movement scholars call "abeyance strategies" that keep their organizations alive and somewhat visible during historical stretches of social
movement doldrums.[2] For instance, a scene I have witnessed scores of
times over the past five years comes to mind: a small handful of ageing
VFP members in Santa Fe, New Mexico, steadfastly maintaining their
Friday street-corner peace vigil, week after week, year after year, their
VFP banners whipping in the wind. Even during the COVID-19 pandemic, still, they persisted: masked, socially distanced, and flashing the
peace sign at passing cars.

In her speech, DeBarros honored this sort of committed "holding of space"
by longtime activists. But she suggested that the movement doldrums were
now ending, that activists were on the cusp of something qualitatively different. Half a year later, DeBarros's speech was revealed as prescient, as social
justice activism exploded in the United States—much of it led by younger
women, people of color, and LGBTQ2S people. A decade or more of community organizing and public education by activists in Black Lives Matter,
climate change, #MeToo, queer, trans and migrant justice work had built a
vibrant social movement network. It took the double spark of a global pandemic and the police murder of George Floyd to ignite widespread action in
what Brittany DeBarros, a few months earlier, had called "broad social justice spaces" that were operating in "unprecedently intersectional" ways. And
it stands to reason that DeBarros could "see" these movement possibilities,
even before the 2020 ignition, because she had not been siloed in a single
veterans' peace organization; rather, she had one foot firmly in About Face's

work against war and militarism, while also stepping into an array of social justice activism around gender, race, and migrant justice issues.

As I witnessed the explosion of social justice activism in the spring and summer of 2020, I wondered: Is it possible that right now, right before our eyes, intersectional praxis is moving—to borrow the famous words of Black feminist leader bell hooks—"from margin to center?"[3] Certainly, as sociologist Benita Roth has observed, for many decades Black and Chicana feminists have "organized on their own," eschewing participation in mainstream White feminist organizations, while maintaining critical dialogue with them.[4] What I am suggesting is that right now we might be seeing something different. Might the ascendance of women of color and queer people to positions of centrality and leadership—in About Face, in many social justice organizations, and even to a certain extent in mainstream media and political commentary—signal a new moment, when previously marginalized "others" are no longer outsiders-within, but rather, are becoming the central drivers of movement praxis grounded in intersectionality? I have argued in this book that the situated knowledge of women of color and LGBTQ2S veterans, derived from their collective experiences "at the margins," fuels an organically intersectional orientation toward social movement praxis. What might intersectional praxis look like, if it truly moves from marginal critique to the center where it becomes the driving force of movement organizations and coalitions?

Border-crossing, or movement silos?

In *Unconventional Combat*, I have drawn from participant observation (some of it in person, some of it in virtual spaces), and I have occasionally brought in the voices of some of the older members of VFP, most of them White men. But I have purposely centered the book's narrative on the words and stories of a group of younger women of color and LGBTQ2S veterans. I show in Chapter 2 that their past experiences—during their youth and especially during their time in the military—shaped a collective, situated knowledge of the ways that militarism intersects with the violences of race, social class, gender, and sexuality. As such, these veterans carry an organic, experience-based intersectional knowledge into their work with Veterans For Peace and About Face. The older membership of VFP, I observed, is committed to building diversity in their organization, including recruiting younger people of color into leadership. However, the collective-knowledge standpoint of the older members—politically radical and anti-war, but still grounded largely in experiences of being White, men, and heterosexual within systems that privilege those statuses—too often fails to move beyond "diversity" to full inclusion of previously marginalized others. The younger cohort of veterans' stories reveal, as I show in Chapter 3, how "diversity" efforts too often fall short within VFP (and sometimes too in About Face), due to the ways that gendered racism subjects them to tokenism, microaggressions, gaslighting, negative assumptions about their leadership abilities, and double standards concerning emotional expression.

The intersectional knowledge of the younger generation of veterans also shapes their views on how VFP and About Face should engage in coalitions with other progressive organizations. As I show in Chapter 4, with intersectionality as the driving force of their praxis, these younger veterans are critical of what they see as the "siloed" nature of VFP, especially its tendency to retain a narrow focus on "the mission" of anti-militarism. Rather, the younger vets favor a fluid coalitional praxis that nimbly shifts toward what is most salient in the political moment, while always carrying with them an understanding of intersectional connections. The shift away from single-issue, single-identity, and brick-and-mortar-based movement organizations is, according to sociologist Dana Fisher, elemental to the emergent field of progressive activism. The "merging of movements" among groups like Black Lives Matter, Occupy, feminists, and anti-gun activists, according to Fisher, is a promising development, but she also emphasizes that "bonds among these movements . . . are fragile."[5] Geographically diffuse, loosely connected, often non-hierarchically coordinated, and connected through social media, these movement networks have the ability to mobilize quickly and broadly. But these same assets may also make it difficult to sustain the existence and work of organizations that is often so necessary for the long haul.

In her intellectual history of intersectionality, political scientist Ange-Marie Hancock asserts that "intersectionality's border-crossing (or traveling, as others put it) is always incomplete, and shot through with politics."[6] In *Unconventional Combat*, I have focused not so much on intersectionality as an intellectual project that crosses academic borders; rather, I have focused on a group of "border crossers" whose intersectional praxis challenges older social movement practices, while promising new directions. But the experiences of these border-crossers is not only "shot through with politics," it tends also to be exhausting for the "travelers" themselves. In the final pages of this chapter, I will explore the emergent tensions in the rise of intersectional praxis in veterans' peace organizations: However promising it is for the larger social movement field, it is by no means clear what it portends for the futures of organizations like VFP and About Face. Will they survive in their current forms? Will they change and adapt to the emergent social movement field? If they do not survive, how will the critical praxis of anti-militarism be fully articulated in the larger social movement field?

Navigating the social movement landscape

Each of my longitudinal interviews with the six veterans on whom I center my analysis in this book spanned anywhere from six months to more than a year.[7] In the context of their continuing lives, this is not a long span of time. But my periodic interviews with each of them revealed shifts and changes in their political practices and priorities, including in their levels of involvement or commitments with VFP or About Face. As I write now, each of their personal trajectories continue, and each will undoubtedly shift further in the future. Here, I reflect especially on how these six are navigating their relationships with VFP and About Face in light of the larger ecology of social movements, during an historical moment of intensifying social movement ferment.

The younger veterans' relationships and strategies with VFP or About Face falls along a continuum. On one end of the continuum, they may choose to engage deeply with these organizations and work with others to change them. When I first started this study in 2018–2019, several of the younger activists I was interviewing and observing seemed to have two feet firmly in VFP and/or About Face, and were determined to work with others to transform them. On the other end of the continuum, the younger activists may decide quit VFP or About Face, and place their energies in other groups or coalitions that are more congruent with their intersectional proclivities. There is a history of this: for instance, of women of color and of lesbians, frustrated with the White, middle-class, and heterosexual basis and bias of the mainstream women's movement, leaving and sometimes forming their own organizations.[8]

Between the opposite poles of full-on engagement with or resignation from veterans' peace organizations, is a third, hybrid strategy: Younger activists can decide to pull back from primary work with VFP and About

Face, instead nimbly shifting their energies to current eruptions of intersectional activism, while still remaining pragmatically connected with VFP or About Face, and strategically bridging anti-militarist praxis with other social movements. During the time of my study, each of the people I focus on in this book migrated along this continuum, most of them moving toward this third, hybrid option. Here, I will briefly profile each of these veterans.

***

Wendy Barranco. Ranging from her 2018–2019 protest, arrest, and trial at the U.S.–Mexico border, her several weeklong trips to staff a health clinic for migrant people in Tijuana, and her rapid mobilization of colleagues in Los Angeles to help poor people meet the challenges the 2020 COVID-19 crisis, Wendy Barranco spent the last two years in a blur of social justice action. Along the way, she told me, "I also started a firearms-training for self-defense, for women of color, for brown folks or black folks." Speaking of her action at the border, she said, "I go down there, I wear the [About Face] t-shirt," but the border action and most of her other recent work, she told me, was conducted independently, at best loosely connected with veterans' peace organizations. For the time being, Barranco sees little reason to work closely with Veterans For Peace. Of VFP's older White male membership, Barranco has concluded,

> They refuse to let go of the baton. They refuse to take a step back and cede leadership, all the while complaining that their membership is dying. "Where are the young veterans? Why won't they come in? Why won't they take over?" They tokenize and they bring you in and they chew you up and then they spit you out. I think until they wrestle with actually ceding leadership, getting out of their own way, nothing is going to change.

About Face, by contrast, has been doing "something radical," letting women (and people of color) lead. Especially since Brittany DeBarros ascended to a leadership position, Barranco says, that organization is heading in the right direction. Still, she sees most of her work for the foreseeable future as flexibly moving toward what is needed at the moment, and organizations seem to impede rather than facilitate that flexible strategy: "I see a gap, I try to fill it in with what I have, and what I bring to the table." She expects that her activism will remain loosely aligned with About Face.

In the last year I've grown out of the space of About Face. It was largely too out of the veteran box. I existed in that box for so long, that's not enough anymore. I have to think about who I am as a woman, who I am as an Indigenous woman, who I am as queer, who I am as brown—all of that—as poor, right? And advancing that in our different movements, and creating those relationships so that folks understand that there are anti-war vets out here with a more nuanced knowledge, and that we're not towing that line of, "I'm proud of my service." I think I, like other women of color, I've just been looking at our experiences with organizations period, and been like, "Fuck this, we're out. We're just going to do our own fricking thing." We just need to be doing our own shit, but also be in synergy with each other, right? I have Britt [DeBarros] on my radar, and I have several other folks on my radar, but we're moving in our own spheres.

Women of color, Barranco emphasizes, are emerging as leaders in a broad-based social justice movement. But this shift is not happening without some organizational strains and tensions.

I think women of color have been the canaries in the coal mine across many movements. We saw Trump coming a mile away and we kept talking about genocide, genocide, genocide. I think folks want to be like, "No." One, they're not listening. Two, I think folks can't grasp that perhaps we might have something of value to say. Perhaps we could have some foresight on these things.

It is time, Barranco concluded, for social movements and society in general to move in fundamentally new directions. "We can't use the same linear thinking. You've got to do something radical. And something radical is like, let women lead, period."

***

Phoenix Johnson. During the summer and fall of 2019, Phoenix Johnson moved full steam-ahead as president of the Seattle Veterans For Peace chapter. Johnson was feeling proud—"I'm pretty sure I'm the only Native American woman to be a chapter lead for Veterans For Peace"—and also optimistic that their chapter had just launched a regular radio show that reached the larger Seattle Metro area. Johnson was also developing a creative strategy for facilitating a generational transition from a chapter made up predominantly of older White men, to a more diverse group of post-9/11 vets.

Phoenix Johnson had already observed the tendency of younger veterans—especially women, queer, and BIPOC (Black, Indigenous, People of Color) ones—to briefly check-in with a VFP chapter, experience alienation, and rapidly drop out. Johnson developed an innovative "outside-in" recruitment and chapter-building strategy. Instead of immediately inviting younger vets of color into VFP spaces, Johnson first "built the capacity outside of the group. I've created basically a reservoir for post-9/11 veterans through meet and greets, happy hours, or a dinner. I have a private online forum through Facebook, where I've built the group [of] veterans who are mostly of diverse identity. I would say between ten and fifteen of them have completed their membership process." Johnson planned to build community among this young, diverse cohort of vets, while preparing them for what to expect when they joined VFP:

> Quite straight up, I said, "These folks are aged White folks with a couple of civilians," so their mentality is as such. They do not have the same diversity, they do not have the same experiences, and they're definitely well-intentioned people, they're enthusiastic, and kind, and welcoming. That doesn't mean that they're not going to say problematic shit, because they have.

Johnson dreamed of going national with this transitional program, reviving dying VFP chapters, and starting new ones with a diverse generation of post-9/11 vets. Some older VFP vets were supportive, including an 85-year-old man in the Seattle chapter who told Johnson, "We are dying. We're not going to be here after so many years. I'm getting tired. I'm going to step back. When we do that, what is going to happen to Veterans For Peace? I don't want it to die with us. We're going to have to pass this on." Still, the recruitment strategy hit bumps. Johnson's vision of several post-9/11 vets showing up en masse and eventually assuming leadership of the chapter didn't materialize. Instead, a few new recruits began to show up to chapter meetings in ones and twos, "and they would say immediately, 'That's not for me,' because incidences would happen with the older regime where they would be patronizing, or other ways of subtle microaggressions of sexism or racism."

A single parent with low income, Phoenix Johnson shares an experience of economic precarity with many post-9/11 vets. By contrast, the older White members of VFP, Johnson says, typically have a "two-story home you've owned for the past 40 years, and your RV and two separate cars." Still, some members of their chapter objected to Johnson receiving an honorarium for a public speech delivered in Johnson's capacity as VFP chapter president. When the pandemic hit in the spring of 2020, "everything got kicked into neutral" in Johnson's VFP chapter. For Johnson and other younger vets, the resulting economic downturn only served to exacerbate existing class distinctions between the VFP old guard and the post-9/11 vets.

> We have post-9/11 [vets] who are economically disadvantaged. We have mental health concerns that are different, that are not being addressed. We have larger gender diversity. It's important to have frank conversations on why it's important to compensate people like me. There's literally no way to exist without that support. Sleep and shelter are basic needs. We can't exist, but we also can't even do the work. I found myself saying, "This group was established in privilege."

In June 2020, "frustrated with some of the dynamics" in their chapter, Johnson delivered a letter to chapter members and to the national VFP office, resigning as chapter president. In the five-page letter—also signed "in resignation and solidarity" by a dozen post-9/11 vets whom Johnson had recruited for the Seattle VFP chapter—Johnson wrote, "I say with a heavy heart that Veterans For Peace is not an organization that truly values veterans of diversity. The antiwar movement is not the peace and justice movement I was led to believe it was." In an interview with Johnson a month after sending this letter, I was told that Johnson had not fully resigned from VFP, and they were continuing to dialogue with the national leadership about organizational priorities. Johnson suggested to VFP, for instance, that the organization should reconsider "dumping thousands and thousands" of dollars into maintaining and supporting *The Golden Rule*, VFP's "peace boat" that for many years has sailed to destinations around the world to promote peace.[9] I asked Johnson what VFP should spend its resources on instead. "Oh, my gosh," Johnson replied, "We could actually be putting it into more effective campaigns around current events such as the demilitarization and defunding of the police. We could actually be doing a nationwide campaign and even a tour to talk about specific examples of how civil police are militarized." Just the previous day, Johnson lamented, a Black Lives Matter protestor in Seattle had been run over and killed by a right-wing terrorist in a car. Johnson would be going out that night to help build security for social justice activists in the street. This would not be a VFP action, Johnson clarified, but when putting their body on the line later that night, Johnson would, as always, be "strategically using that veteran status."

***

Monique Salhab. When I first met them in the winter of 2019, Monique Salhab had recently left their position as a national board member for Veterans For Peace, but had remained active in the organization, including in the VFP chapter in Albuquerque, New Mexico. A few months later, Salhab resigned from the Albuquerque chapter while retaining a national VFP membership. Salhab continues to believe that VFP has an important role to play and worries that the organization is currently on a trajectory just to shrivel and die. "I don't want to see that," they emphasized, "I don't want that happening." But Salhab had become frustrated with VFP's inability or unwillingness to "connect the dots" in ways that reflect the experiences and perspectives of a younger and more diverse cohort of veterans.

> In my experience, I didn't feel like there was a tangible bridge in trying to create some intergenerational connections. With an organization that was founded by White men and that is still White male led, there has been no true—I'll say *conscientious*—honoring of how to make space for women, for women of color, for queer, trans. And to recognize what we can bring, how we are taking activism to a new level. Meaning constant conversations about decolonization. Decolonization is about addressing the colonizer, it's about addressing imperialism. It's about addressing the military. Talking about queer and trans folk is about dealing with the inequality and costs of war to individuals who serve, [who] then get out and don't have tangible access to health care from the VA, that a heterosexual person has. Having people of color means talking about how the terrorism that we talk about going on overseas, that the military brings to other countries, is about the reality, that terror, that people of color face in their own communities here in the United States by law enforcement, which receives equipment from the military surplus program.

A point of no return in Monique Salhab's struggles with their VFP chapter was when they suggested that the group stop using the term "minority," and instead adopt the newer term "BIPOC." Salhab was shocked that the suggestion drew an "overwhelming amount of backlash from majority White men. And no joke: I had one email that said, 'Fuck you. You're a fucking minority. Deal with it.' There's no reason at all why I should be receiving emails like this. No reason. And it just got worse. And so finally, I was like, 'You know what? I'm done.'"

As for About Face, Salhab has "a lot of respect for the organization." Salhab had recently participated in a Zoom discussion that included about fifteen VFP and About Face leaders. One man, Salhab said, "got really excited. He was just, 'I think it would be great to have a merger, VFP and About Face.'" On the one hand, Salhab liked the idea of how a merger would create an intergenerational connection between the older VFP and younger About Face vets. "Wouldn't it be beautiful to have this coming together?" But Salhab also cautiously suggested that such a merger may be more beneficial for VFP than for About Face. "I was like, 'I sort of feel like About Face could school VFP on a lot.' And I said, 'I don't know. Would About Face as an organization really feel like that is a good thing?'" A merger may sound attractive, Salhab told colleagues, "But there's everything else that comes with that." In VFP, Salhab told them, "You have members who, when us younger vets talk about some of these intersecting ideas, who say that we're distracting from the work of VFP. So they don't even see the connection of things."

Monique Salhab may be done with their VFP chapter but is far from done with activist work. They continue their work with social justice coalitions in Albuquerque (Figure 5.1). And in the spring and summer of 2020, Salhab spoke in a series of online webinars about militarization and racial justice. When doing so, speaking publicly as a veteran and as a member of VFP, Salhab contributed a critical understanding of militarization, adding a unique dimension to community discussions of police violence and racial justice. Salhab told me that "I don't need to be a part of the chapter to do work around veterans' issues and all the things that are attached to that. I know VFP can do better. I also believe VFP has to do better. But then the flip side of that is, I can only do what I can do. I will continue to do that work, and I'll continue to work on the boundaries of VFP, right?"

∗∗∗

Monisha Ríos. In January 2020, Monisha Ríos moved to Vieques, Puerto Rico. Ríos intends to say there for the long haul, she told me, working with "my people" doing "class work" to fight against "austerity measures that are happening in Puerto Rico, the ongoing cultural genocide of Puerto

Figure 5.1 Monique Salhab speaking at the 2018 Women's March, Albuquerque, NM
Photo courtesy of Monique Salhab

Rico as well as just settler colonialism." A big part of the pain of the Puerto Rican people in Vieques, Ríos says, is due to the toxic legacy of the island's use by the U.S. military for air bases, bombing ranges, chemical and biological weapons testing, and depleted uranium dumping.[10] Ríos's family, she told me, had participated in past protests in Vieques, and the land she was now living on had been "reclaimed from the Navy."

The work Ríos was launching in Puerto Rico was both academic—she was working on a doctoral dissertation—and political. For the previous two or three years, Ríos had tried to bridge VFP with Psychologists for Social Responsibility (PSR), to build a coalition to "demilitarize psychology." Her interest in fusing a scholarly critique of militarized psychology with political action was sparked by her experiences as a veteran who struggled to receive services for military sexual trauma.

My [research] design [starts with] all the work I've done since I first began investigating the ethics of the industry, from the standpoint of being an MST survivor, trying to secure the VA, and seeing firsthand how, not only on active duty, psychologists are complicit in covering up sex crimes, but

also within the VA system. And so that's where my investigation began, out
of necessity, and part of that movement.

She concluded that VFP members had little interest in this topic, so she
had recently shifted the locus of her work to PSR, an organization with a rich
legacy of exposing the complicity of professional psychologists in support of
U.S. torture, a practice that escalated during the early years of the U.S. war
in Iraq under President George W. Bush. In 2020, Monisha Ríos was elected
president of PSR, likely the first veteran to hold that position. Once she
arrived in Puerto Rico, Ríos's research expanded into an "autoethnographic
study" of the impact of militarized psychology "from the perspective of the
colonized people" who had been targeted by U.S. wars and settler colonialism. With the research, Ríos plans to build public awareness and critical
dialogue, in hopes of expanding the work into a full-on inquiry into the militarization and weaponization of psychology in the United States, how it's
used, and who is used upon, what are the impacts of that on an individual's
families, communities, the environment. And then build from there, and
maybe one day see a people's tribunal of U.S. military psychology occur.
That's the number one goal.

Monisha Ríos remains loosely connected with VFP, however she told me
that over the past few months, she had arrived "almost to the point of saying
'fuck this,' renouncing my lifetime membership. And just not having anything to do with the organization, but still working with individuals and
chapters who are doing their own work." She says VFP needs to "spend more
time doing that internal work, that healing, addressing the toxic masculinity,
misogyny, addressing the internal racism, cleaning house." Ríos remains
hopeful about VFP, which she believes "could actually be a benefit to the
peace movement," but she has concluded that her own time and energies will
be better spent elsewhere. With a light chuckle, she told me,

> I don't see myself as anything more than like a small potato, so I don't know
> that VFP would really suffer without me. I think VFP is looking at its own
> death, its own demise. I don't feel like my work is fixing VFP. My work is
> exposing the military psychological industrial complex, and you know,
> doing anti-imperialist work. And fixing VFP is not that. There has to be a
> line that we draw for ourselves, where we choose to take care of ourselves.
> And I think that's where Monique [Salhab] is at. And I think we're both in
> the same place on that, at this point.

Figure 5.2 Monisha Ríos (lower right) with About Face panel on the political future of Puerto Rico, October 2020
Screen shot by author

In the spring of 2020, Monisha Ríos found a fresh alignment, joining with About Face members Jovanni Reyes and Camilo Mejia for a webinar series that explored multiple dynamics of psychological warfare. The three have "a little affinity group among ourselves," Ríos said, "We are all Latin American." And she contributed to another About Face webinar in October 2020 on the political future of Puerto Rico (Figure 5.2). Ríos appreciates how About Face has been "trying to create space to be more inclusive with membership." I asked Ríos if she expects VFP to be involved in her future work. "No," she replied, "because I don't want it to be." She paused, adding, "And eventually, yes, I will be selectively involved."

***

Stephen Funk. On June 20, 2020, President Donald Trump held an ill-fated campaign rally in Tulsa Oklahoma, during a moment of rising COVID-19 cases in Oklahoma. On that morning I noticed that Stephen Funk posted on social media that he was "Protesting Patriarchy in Tulsa." Later that day, Funk posted a short video from outside the stunningly empty area about which Trump had boasted in advance that it would be teeming with thousands of his supporters. Two weeks later, I asked Stephen Funk about his counter-protest action in Tulsa, implying that I was a bit surprised because I was under the impression that Funk had recently pulled back from activist work. He bristled a bit at my assumption, reminding me in an email that activism has always been a part of his life.

> I've been organizing activism since middle school when we organized a walkout at my school called "skirt fest" because a boy got expelled for wearing a skirt to class. And I went to a progressive high school where we protested the WTO [World Trade Organization]. In S.F., I organized Veteran Artists. I've been involved with IVAW/About Face to various degrees over the years. I was in Tulsa, and it was hilariously empty. I was officially there with About Face who organized transportation super last minute which was fun; our group gets called upon to "deploy" and are rather efficient at mobilizations.

My errant assumption that Funk had pulled back from activism was likely based on some thoughts he had shared with me in recent interviews. In particular, Funk had expressed concern that he did not want his generation of post-9/11 veterans to find themselves "living a frozen life," as many older members of VFP have, in Funk's view.

> I've seen it in the Vietnam generation where there's veterans who weave a story around themselves, and get trapped by it, and they don't really have a desire to add to it. It's like a nostalgia story that freezes them. People are comfortable there. But it's also like, that's when they were their most alive and most happy or something. And they want that to be their life forever, the time when they really did feel the most alive. They were at war, that's the experience. And then they get back and they're protesting the war. And during the Vietnam era everything was extreme. Everything was an experience. And so they don't want to leave. They feel like that is the epicenter for their life and they'd never want to grow up.

Funk has a different vision for himself and for post-9/11 veterans. "My hope for veterans in my generation is that they use their story to propel them forward to continue to have an interesting story. And to create opportunities for themselves, and to not be stuck in a closed circle of a story that never grows larger." In the winter of 2020, Funk told me that even though About Face was smaller and less visible than it had been ten or fifteen years earlier, he was pleased to see the ascent of women and men of color and queer people into positions of leadership. For Funk, About Face continues to be a flexible vehicle for his generational cohort to "propel them forward."

During the height of the Iraq War, Funk recalls, he had been part of a "surge of people" engaged in a flurry of anti-war activism with IVAW. In the current moment, he told me during the winter of 2020, that kind of mass activism didn't seem to "make sense." Instead, he saw About Face operating as a kind of "think tank. It's like there's a knowledge base at this point. You can have a strong, small, lean organization that meets the moment." What he appreciated most about IVAW/About Face, Funk told me, is that it does not have a singular focus, that it is instead a flexible locus for "a lot of creative offshoots" of activist work. A few months after Funk praised About Face's "small, lean" organizational flexibility during a time of apparent movement doldrums, the organization seemed to prove his points. As mass racial justice activism erupted in the spring and summer, About Face quickly pivoted, presenting numerous online forums on racial justice and the militarization of policing, and mobilizing several actions, including the Trump counter-protest that Funk joined in Tulsa.

***

Brittany Ramos DeBarros. There is a good deal of cautious optimism among veterans concerning the future of About Face, due in part to the recent leadership provided by Brittany Ramos DeBarros. She and others are consciously building a flexible organization that organically links veterans' anti-war, anti-militarism perspectives into a growing movement for social justice for which intersectionality is its driving praxis. As the story at the outset of this chapter shows, DeBarros remains connected with VFP, but after watching other women of color work within VFP, she has decided for the moment that "I'm not going to be another person who spins my wheels and gets chewed up" by VFP.

> Monique [Salhab] and Monisha [Ríos] were organizing within the movement, you know. I just thought that all that energy and their brilliance had been basically squandered, trying to shift VFP an inch. It's a shame, and I developed an analysis at that point, that that wasn't the best strategy for us at this point. I also was very rapidly getting clearer and clearer on a perspective, that the existing anti-war institutional infrastructure that we had was a net negative, in my opinion, and I still mostly think that.

When people suggest the possibility of VFP and About Face merging, DeBarros replies that she still feels "hopeful" about VFP. "I continue to engage with them." However, she emphasizes,

> I'm really kind of bluntly transparent with them where I'm just like, "It's hard for us right now to be really publicly aligned with you all, because your base acts crazy. But I just want to let you know, I'm committed to working with you and I believe in you as people, like what you're trying to do there." But [the idea of] aligning About Faces' brand with VFPs brand? Do you value About Faces' brand? For example, right now, one of the strongest things I think About Face has developed is really deep relationships with diaspora communities. And that exists in VFP too, but the collective practice is not there to maintain trust.

Meanwhile, DeBarros and her About Face colleagues began the summer of 2020 growing as an organization and demonstrating what a veterans' anti-war organization can bring to an erupting mass movement. In a mid-July online fundraising message, DeBarros noted that in recent weeks, About Face had added 150 new members and had engaged in an impressive range of actions and campaigns, which she went on to list:[11]

> Organized a National Guard Stand-down mini-campaign in response to anti-protest mobilizations; Worked with the Movement for Black Lives, Working Families party and Vets For the People to launch a #VetsForBlackLives mini-campaign; Mobilized dozens of members across the nation to leverage their skills as street medics and community security during uprisings in several cities; Joined the call to close down Ft. Hood in response to Vanessa Guillen's brutal murder and ongoing abuses of the military to women, especially women of color; Participated in the Poor People's Campaign as one of the main voices against militarism; Mobilized to support Black and Indigenous organizers in disrupting Trump's first campaign rally during Juneteenth in Tulsa; Became a key partner in the call to defund the Pentagon and support the current legislation to reduce the Department of Defense budget by at least 10%; and supported the Lakota Treaty Protectors at Six Grandfathers (Mt. Rushmore) in which two members were arrested denying Trump access to sovereign lands.

"The work will go on"

Over time, social movement organizations, including veterans' peace organizations, tend to ebb and flow. Some surge during times of rapid social
change—as did Vietnam Veterans against the War, during the 1960s and early
1970s—only to shrink back, or even disappear, when movement activism
recedes. Other organizations, such as VFP and About Face over the past
decade, may contract in size during such times, but with core members remaining active—engaging in what social movement scholars call "abeyance
strategies"[12] or what Brittany DeBarros described as "holding space . . . to
keep the flame alive."

This seemed an apt description of both VFP and About Face. Each organization experienced booming membership numbers and boasted an
impressive range of activities between 2004 and 2008, during the height of
the U.S. wars in Iraq and Afghanistan. By the time I started the research for
this book in 2018 and 2019, both organizations' size and scope of activities
had been contracting for several years. However, the COVID-19 pandemic
and the mass uprisings for racial justice in 2020 created a serendipitous research opportunity for me, to observe VFP's and About Face's organizational
responses in this rapidly shifting field. It will come of little surprise to scholars
of social movements that About Face, the group with younger members, was
especially nimble in shifting much of their work to online activism during the
early weeks of the pandemic. As sociologist Alison Crossley has observed,
younger activists tend to view both online activism and in-person activism
as necessary and as mutually reinforcing dimensions of contemporary social
movement work.[13]

What surprised me was the ways in which VFP, an organization with
much older membership, also shifted gears during the pandemic and found
ways to contribute to the racial justice uprisings. After a brief hiatus, the
Santa Fe, New Mexico, VFP chapter I am affiliated with continued its longstanding Friday peace vigil. That chapter had also been working in conjunc-
tion with the Albuquerque chapter and the national office to plan the 2020
VFP national convention for August, to coincide with larger mobilizations in
nearby Los Alamos to commemorate the 75th anniversary of the U.S. atomic
bombings of Hiroshima and Nagasaki, and to protest continuing development of nuclear arms at the site. I attended Zoom-based chapter meetings,
portions of which each month were focused on discussions of shifting plans

to hold the national convention entirely online. This was a major disappointment, especially as it undercut the plan for drawing huge numbers of people to Los Alamos for an in-person protest against nuclear weapons development, but the VFP planners drew up an online convention program that continued to highlight that issue and included an appropriately diverse list of speakers, including Native American activists who work against the appropriation of Indigenous peoples' lands for plutonium mining and nuclear testing. The VFP chapter also, each month, discussed "how can we be of service," both to the local Black Lives Matter movement and to youth-led climate justice activists.

Older VFP members are painfully aware that their organization is not growing and that the membership is rapidly ageing. They are also aware that some younger veterans—especially women of color leaders—have pulled back from their involvement in VFP. Vic, a VFP member in his 80s, lamented, "I've poured a lot of energy and time and frankly money into Veterans For Peace over the years, so I'd like to see it continue." The future of VFP, he thinks, lies in "whether a path forward can be developed with About Face." If a merger with About Face does not happen, "I think otherwise, we'll see that gradually, will the last vet turn out the lights?" Another longtime VFP member, Mac, shrugged his shoulders when I asked him about the future of VFP. "These organizations have their period," he said, and "if About Face does not take over VFP, it will just fade away." Michael, another older VFP activist seems equally philosophical: "Whether VFP survives or not, the work will go on," he said.

The six younger veterans whose stories I foreground in *Unconventional Combat* maintain a thin thread of connection with VFP. Their respect for the decades of committed peace and justice work done by older VFP members shines through in their hope that VFP members will "do the work" that is necessary for VFP to evolve into an organization driven by intersectional praxis. Clearly though, these individuals have decided it is not their job to reform VFP. Instead, some of them are working with one foot in About Face, and the other foot stepping into one, then another, currently salient social movement context. Ranging from racial justice, to climate justice, to migrant justice, to gender and sexual justice and anti-colonial actions, their praxis is driven by their collective, experience-based intersectionality. As they move about the larger social movement field, these veterans carry the VFP and About Face mission of anti-militarism into each and every one of these social justice efforts. Brittany DeBarros neatly summarized this goal: "We actually don't need to build a new separate anti-war movement," she asserted. "We need to build the capacity for anti-militarist analysis within the broader social justice canon that is already being realized across social justice spaces and across the society."

***

There has been a great deal of cross-talk among progressives for decades, with various groups laying claims to define "the challenge of our times." Climate change. Global pandemics. Racial injustice. Colonial domination. Gender and sexual violence. War and militarism. The promise of the new generation of progressive activists lies in their great refusal to pick and choose one or the other of these issues, claiming it to be now and always the center of progressive activism. When I was a budding young radical in the early 1970s, one of my Marxist professors told me that no matter what issue a movement was focused on—racism, sexism, environmental destruction— eventually "all roads lead to the Primary Contradiction: capitalism." As I have suggested in this book, intersectional praxis reveals this sort of reductionist thinking to be limiting, even self-destructive. Intersectional praxis presses social movements beyond the confines of such linear, reductionist thinking, revealing that no matter which particular issue is at the center of current progressive activism, everything is interconnected and mutually constitutive: all roads lead to coalition politics.

As Brittany DeBarros's words suggest, today's "emergent social justice spaces" are driven by intersectional praxis. The knowledge underlying this praxis bubbles up from the collective experiences of systemic oppression, violence and suffering shared by women, LGBTQ2S, Black, Indigenous, and People of Color; intersectionality crystalizes as praxis in the political/intellectual work of generations of women of color scholar-activists. Today, younger activists like the six military veterans I focus on in this book are importing this collective knowledge into organizations and social movements, and they are pressing intersectional praxis to the center of strategies to change the world.

Intersectional praxis was, of course, not invented by anti-war military veterans. But, as I have shown in this book, veterans bring to social justice coalitions a crucial understanding of the ways that war and militarism both feed on and in turn generate institutional racism, colonial domination, injustice for migrants, gender and sexual violence, environmental destruction, and climate change. The VFP and About Face members I focus on in this book lamented to me many times about the dearth of a critical analysis of war and militarism in many of the social justice organizations they contribute to. For this reason alone, the continuing existence of a visible veterans' peace and justice organization—be it VFP, or About Face, or some hybrid re-formation of these organizations—is crucially important in the years and decades ahead.

The older generation of activists in VFP continue steadfastly to oppose war and militarism. They have been, as Brittany DeBarros said, "creating the space . . . holding the space, through decades of invisibility, of uphill battles." The longtime members of VFP may now be writing the final chapters in their long lives of peace activism, but they have not yet closed the book. In the fall of 2020, as I was putting *Unconventional Combat* to bed, members of the Santa Fe and Albuquerque VFP chapters invited me to present some of the ideas in the book to them. In a Zoom meeting attended mostly by older White men and women, I found these longtime VFP members to be both curious and open to the self-reflexive critical dialogue that I hope this book will help to stimulate and perhaps facilitate. The future of veterans' peace and justice organizations will undoubtedly be driven by the intersectional praxis of a diverse generational cohort of post-9/11 veterans. In the immediate future, the continuing story of veterans' peace and justice organizations will be shaped in part by progressive veterans' intergenerational dialogue.

Centering Intersectional Standpoints

In *Unconventional Combat,* I have placed the stories and voices of six military veterans—all people of color, three of them women, one an Indigenous Two-Spirit person, one a genderqueer non-binary person, and three who identify as queer—at the center of my analysis. I argue that their social locations at the junctures of systems of race, gender, social class, sexual and colonial violence and oppression—both inside and outside the military—subjected them to experiences that generated shared knowledge, a collective standpoint through which they forge political theory and action, an intersectional praxis.

To say that I am "centering" this diverse group of veterans' intersectional standpoint is not the same as to claim that I have "adopted" this standpoint as my own. In fact, as a sociologist whose experience is situated at the nexus of multiple systems of privilege, it would be worse than merely arrogant for me to make this claim. I am not a veteran. Moreover, I am an older, White, heterosexually identified man who enjoys financial security as a tenured professor. This should raise questions for a reader: How has my social location of privilege shaped my knowledge? How might my positionality have impacted the willingness of people of color, women, or queer veterans to speak with me? What might I miss, or perhaps distort the meanings of, in listening to life histories of people from very different backgrounds who are sharing stories with me about their experiences of sexual assault, gendered racism, financial precarity, homophobia, or the trauma of war? It is in the very nature of these questions that I cannot answer them with complete confidence. But here, in the spirit of critical self-reflexivity, I will share some observations about the research, and some strategies I deployed to create and sustain critical dialogue with the six veterans who invested their time and trust in me, and in my project.

Working on *Unconventional Combat* is not the first time I have taken on the task of interviewing people who are different from me. I have done life history interviews with male former athletes who are gay, Black, Latino, or of poor working-class origin. I have interviewed a diverse group of women who work as volunteer youth sports coaches. And in a project that focused mostly on men who work as "feminist allies" in preventing gender-based violence, I also interviewed a racially and sexually diverse group of women who work with these men. In all of these studies, I have sought to ask feminist intersectional questions. Doing this kind of work means, at its base, listening to women, reading and drawing critical ideas from scholarly work by women and people of color, and using these ideas as a foundation from which to ask questions about the workings of power and inequality. But the devil is often in the details; the question of *which* women to listen to can never be answered finally, with some set formula. Instead, it requires an ongoing process of reflexivity that includes interrogating the ways that one's own privileged standpoint, however "progressive" or "intersectional" its intent, will retain some blind spots if it is not in continual dialogue with differently situated people.

As I began the work for *Unconventional Combat,* I tried to keep these principles in mind, and the individuals I interviewed consistently helped me to do so. Still, it was not always easy to secure the agreement of VFP or About Face women of color and/or queer vets to participate. For instance, I tried multiple times, and failed, to interview three other women of color whose stories I believed would have enhanced my research. Two initially said yes, then backed out before the first interview. I was told that one was "pulling back from her work" with the organization for a time, to engage in some "self-care." Her situation did not surprise me; every woman of color veteran I met seemed to be carrying huge loads of social activism, sometimes while trying to care for a family, and often with very thin financial resources. And though I have no direct evidence of this, it's not hard to imagine that one or more of these veterans who opted out of my study did so due to the social distance they felt from me: Why should they invest their time and trust in this old White guy, when there are so many other important things to do? Indeed, before Wendy Barranco would agree to a life history interview with me, she pointedly asked, "What's in this for you?" And when I met Phoenix Johnson in the hotel lobby at a VFP convention and asked if they would do an interview with me, Johnson looked startled, saying "I'm surprised." When I asked them to explain, Johnson expressed surprise that anyone actually wanted to hear what any of the younger cohort of women of color vets have to say. Johnson told me that "[w]e spend a lot of time yelling to be heard," and then eventually, "people decide they don't like us, because we yell so much."

To build trust, I needed to explain to each of the six why I was interested, what my goals and intentions were. I offered to give each of them a copy of *Guys Like Me,* and it helped that one of the vets I featured in that book, Daniel Craig, and also Wendy Barranco, who was the first person I interviewed for *Unconventional Combat,* introduced me to others, and vouched for me. "Any friend of Wendy's," I was told by two of the others, "is a friend of mine." I explained as best I could "what was in it for me," emphasizing that I don't tend to make money from most of my books—in fact, I'd have to sell a lot of books to earn back the out-of-pocket expenses I pay for research, travel, and creating a website for the book. I also made a modest donation to VFP or About Face, in appreciation for each person's participation in the project. And though I am a senior scholar who no longer needs publications to stand for some future promotion, writing a book does create an intangible benefit for me, of enhancing my scholarly reputation. But mostly, I explained, writing such a book makes me feel better about myself, that I am contributing something to progressive activism. I have never been a deeply engaged on-the-ground activist. Rather, I am scholar who works at the edges of social justice organizations, contributing minimally to the actual work, but hoping that my research can serve in two ways: As critical analysis that might facilitate internal dialogue in and across social justice organizations, and as a way to make the work of these organizations more visible to the general public. My previous book, *Guys Like Me,* I explained, was written and promoted with those goals and intentions.

I am grateful to everyone who agreed to talk with me, formally or informally, as I conducted the research for this book. But I am especially grateful to the six whose stories I foreground in the book. With each of the six, I completed long, audio-recorded interviews, conducted over several months, in several sittings. The first meeting with each person was a lengthy, in-person interview. Subsequent meetings conducted on Zoom were separated by weeks, or sometime by months. In sociological research, most "in-depth interviews," including many I have done in the past, are single snapshots in time; for this project, my revisiting the interviews with these six over the course of nearly a year proved invaluable, allowing me to see changes in individuals' lives, and also in the ways that they were pivoting and altering their priorities and strategies with VFP and/or About Face during a moment of social turbulence due to the global COVID-19 pandemic and resurgent racial justice activism.

As I moved forward with this project, I came to admire each of these individuals' deep commitments to social justice, their sophisticated collective intersectional praxis, and all of the risks and sacrifices they make as activists. As I began to write up the book, it was not difficult, for the most part, for me to "center" their stories. However, there were times when I was tempted to interject the older White men's stories and perspectives as a counter-point to the stories I was hearing from the six. I wondered to what extent my admiration for (and my identification with?) these mostly White men of my generation might be tugging me away from my commitment to center the intersectional stories of the six. I did draw some quotes from these older White men to deepen the context of my analysis, but I consciously avoided falling into a "she said-he said" form of storytelling, a common journalistic practice that tends to create a false symmetry that can ultimately re-marginalize the voices of oppressed groups. The reader can judge the extent to which I succeeded in this effort.

As a form of reflexive dialogue with the six, I deployed some other strategies. First, since I intended to use their real names in the book, I sent each person a copy of the transcribed interviews to give them the opportunity to locate comments or stories that they would rather not see in print. Not all of them did this, ultimately. As I said, these are very busy people, and these transcripts are long. Moreover, each of them had spoken with me about very difficult personal issues—disclosures of sexual assaults, racist or homophobic abuse, combat trauma, drug use, depression, imprisonment—and some just may have found it too difficult to read through these transcripts. Second, I also sent to each person a draft of the profile I wrote about them for Chapter 2. Each of the six read their own profile and sent me small edits to fix errors I might have made. Two asked me to delete a sentence or two that recounted painful stories they decided they would rather not see in print. I made these changes.

As the book went to press, I invited each of the six to give me feedback and to perhaps contribute to the book's companion website, unconventionalcombat.com. The website, I hope, will be a site for continuing dialogue about the issues raised in the book. And finally, I have communicated to these veterans that I intend to use the book as much as I can to make public their work and amplify their voices. So, for instance, when I am invited to make a public presentation about the book, I will endeavor to include one or more of these vets in the event.

Notes

Prologue

1. Ursula K. Le Guin 1973. The ones who walk away from Omelas. In Robert Silverberg, ed., *New Dimensions 3.* Garden City, NY: Nelson Doubleday/SFBC.
2. C. Wright Mills 1959. *The sociological imagination.* New York: Oxford University Press.
3. Simone De Beauvoir 2015 (1948). *The ethics of ambiguity.* New York: Philosophical Library.
4. Naomi Klein 2007. *The shock doctrine: The rise of disaster capitalism.* New York: Metropolitan Books.
5. Patricia Hill Collins 2013. The ethos of violence. Pp. 187–197 in Patricia Hill Collins, ed., *On intellectual activism.* Philadelphia: Temple University Press, quote from p. 190.

Chapter 1

1. Cynthia Enloe 2000. *Maneuvers: The international politics of militarizing women's lives.* Berkeley: University of California Press, p. 3. While Enloe mostly examines the ways that militarization meshes with patriarchy, Catherine Lutz traces militarization's "relationship to broader social changes, from the emergence of nation states to the course of racialization and other inequalities to the convergence of interests in military spending." Catherine Lutz 2002. Making war at home in the United States: Militarization and the current crisis. *American Anthropologist* 104(3): 723–735, quote from p. 723. For a broader critical examination of militarization, see Roberto J. Gonzalez, Hugh Gusterson, & Gustaaf Houtman, eds. 2019. *Militarization: A reader.* Durham & London: Duke University Press.
2. Enloe, 2000, p. 291.
3. Benjamin Schrader 2019. The affect of veteran activism. *Critical Military Studies* 5: 63–77, quote from p. 67.
4. To the more common umbrella term LGBTQ (lesbian, gay, bisexual, trans, queer), I purposefully include "2S" to be inclusive of Indigenous "Two-Spirit" people, one of whom, Phoenix Johnson, is included in the stories I center on in this book. Before the 1990s, anthropologists commonly used the term "Berdache" to refer to the long tradition among many Native peoples to honor a third (or even fourth) gender category in their nations. Around 1990, Native people settled on their own umbrella term, "Two-Spirit," to describe this sex/gender identity. Today, Two-Spirit people are forging spaces as outsiders-within mainstream LGBTQ2S cultures, and also within

Native nations. Qwo-Li Driskill 2016. *Asegi stories: Cherokee queer and Two-Spirit memory.* Tucson: University of Arizona Press; Sarah Hunt 2016. *An introduction to the health of Two-Spirit people: Historical, contemporary and emergent issues.* Prince George, BC: National Collaborating Centre for Aboriginal Health; K. L. Walters, T. Evans-Campbell, J. Wimomi, T. Ronquillo, & R. Bhuyan 2006. "My spirit in my heart": Identity experiences and challenges among American Indian two-spirited women. *Journal of Lesbian Studies 10*: 125–149.

5. Ange-Marie Hancock 2016. *Intersectionality: An intellectual history.* New York: Oxford University Press. Leslie McCall 2005. The complexity of intersectionality. *Signs: Journal of Women in Culture and Society 30*: 1771–1800

6. Catherine Lutz 2004. Living room terrorists: Rates of domestic violence are three to five times higher among military couples than among civilian ones. *Women's Review of Books 21* (5): 17–18.

7. Sarah Ruddick 1989. Mothers and men's wars. Pp. 75–92 in Adrienne Harris & Ynestra King, eds., *Rocking the ship of state: Toward a feminist peace politics.* Boulder, San Francisco, & London: Westview Press. See also Adrienne Harris 1989. Bringing Artemis to life: A plea for militance and aggression in feminist peace politics. Pp. 93–113 in Adrienne Harris & Ynestra King, eds., *Rocking the ship of state: Toward a feminist peace politics;* Kylea Laina Leise 2019. Childbirth in the context of conflict in Afghanistan. Pp. 41–56 in Catherine Lutz & Andrea Mazzarino, eds., *War and health: The medical consequences of the wars in Iraq and Afghanistan.* New York: New York University Press.

8. Sealing Cheng 2013. *On the move for love: Migrant entertainers in the U.S. military in South Korea.* Philadelphia: University of Pennsylvania Press; Cynthia Enloe 1989. *Bananas, beaches and bases: Making feminist sense of international politics.* Berkeley: University of California Press; Enloe, 2000; Philippa Levine 2004. "A multitude of unchaste women": Prostitution in the British Empire. *Journal of Women's History 15* (4): 159–163.

9. Pamela DeLargy 2013. Sexual violence and women's health in war. Pp. 54–79 in Carol Cohn, ed., *Women and wars.* Malden, MA: Polity; Enloe, 2000; Nicola Henry 2016. Theorizing wartime rape: Deconstructing gender, sexuality and violence, *Gender & Society 10*: 44–56; Andrea Mazzarino, Marcial C. Inhorn, & Catherine Lutz 2019. The health consequences of war. Pp. 1–37 in Catherine Lutz & Andrea Mazzarino, eds. 2019. *War and health: The medical consequences of the wars in Iraq and Afghanistan.* New York: New York University Press. Kimberly Theidon 2007. Gender in transition: Common sense, women and war. *Journal of human rights 6*: 453–478. As political scientist Alison Dundes Renteln has outlined, sexual assaults in times of war and political unrest have only recently begun to be addressed by the international community as a legal and human rights issue. Alison Dundes Renteln 2020. A political analysis of sexual violence in the International Criminal Court. Pp. 102–125 in Julie Fraser & Brionne McGonigle Leyh, eds., *Intersections of law and culture at the International Criminal Court.* Cheltenham, UK: Edward Elgar Publisher.

10. For a concise but detailed historical overview of women's roles as nurses in various militaries, see pp. 198–234 in Enloe, 2000.. See also Connie L. Reeves 1996. The

military women's vanguard: Nurses. Pp. 73–114 in Judith Hicks Stiehm, ed., *Our military too! Women and the U.S. military*. Philadelphia: Temple University Press.

11. Robert Egnel & Mayesha Alam, eds. 2019. *Women and gender perspectives in the military: An international comparison*. Washington, DC: Georgetown University Press. Lory Manning 2004. Military women: Who they are, what they do, and why it matters. *Women's Review of Books 21* (5): 7–8.

12. Lourdes Beneria & Rebecca Blank 1989. Women and the economics of military spending. Pp 191–203 in Adrienne Harris & Ynestra King, eds., *Rocking the ship of state: Toward a feminist peace politics*. Boulder, San Francisco, & London: Westview Press; Angela Raven-Roberts 2013. Women and the political economy of war. Pp. 36–53 in Carol Cohn, *Women and wars*. Malden, MA: Polity.

13. Cynthia Enloe 1988. *Does khaki become you? The militarization of women's lives*. London: Harper Collins; Cynthia Enloe 2004. *The curious feminist: Searching for women in a new age of empire*. Berkeley: University of California Press; J. Ann Tickner 2002. Feminist perspectives on 9/11. *International Studies Perspectives 3*: 333–350; Carol Cohn 2013. Women and wars: Toward a conceptual framework. Pp. 1–35 in Carol Cohn, ed., *Women and wars*. Malden, MA: Polity.

14. Robert Egnell & Mayesha Alam 2019. Gender and women in the military: Setting the stage. Pp. 1–21 in Robert Egnell & Mayesha Alam, eds., *Women and gender perspectives in the military: An international comparison*. Washington, DC: Georgetown University Press, p. 1. Since passing that 2000 Resolution, the U.N. Security Council has passed a sequence of resolutions (in 2008, 2009, 2010, and 2011) that address "conflict related sexual violence," HIV/AIDS policies in post-war regions, and eliminating obstacles to women's participation in peace-building. DeLargy, 2013.

15. Robert Egnell & Mayesha Alam, eds. 2019. *Women and gender perspectives in the military: An international comparison*. Washington, DC: Georgetown University Press.

16. The proportion of women in the U.S. Navy (nearly 25%) and Air Force (23%) is the highest in the military. The U.S. Marine Corps is the lowest, at about 10%, with the U.S. Army in the middle, at roughly 17%. George M. Reynolds & Amanda Shendruk 2018. Demographics of the U.S. Military. Council on Foreign Relations, April 24.

17. Reynolds & Sendruk, 2018. A 2011 PEW study reported that 31% of women in the U.S. military were Black and 51% White, compared with 16% and 71% respectively, for men. Proportions of women vs. men service members who identify as Hispanic (13% to 12%), Asian (4% for each) and "mixed/other" (7% to 5%) were closer to equal. Eileen Patton & Kim Parker 2011. Women in the U.S. military: Growing share, distinctive profile. *PEW Social and demographic trends*. PEW Research Center. For a mid-1990s demographic snapshot of women's numbers in the U.S. military, see Judith Hicks Stiehm 1996. Just the facts, ma'am. Pp. 60–70 in Judith Hicks Stiehm, ed., *It's our military too! Women and the U.S. military*. Philadelphia: Temple University Press.

18. Paige Whaley Eager 2014. *Waging gendered wars: U.S. Military women in Afghanistan and Iraq*. London: Routledge; Brenda Opperman 2019. Women and gender in the U.S. military: A slow process of integration. Pp. 113–140 in Robert Egnell & Mayesha Alam, eds., *Women and gender perspectives in the military: An international comparison*. Washington, DC: Georgetown University Press. For an overview of debates

about women in combat roles from the mid-1990s, see Lucinda Joy Peach 1996. Gender ideology and the ethics of women in combat. Pp. 156–194 in Judith Hicks Stiehm, ed., *It's our military too! Women and the U.S. military.* Philadelphia: Temple University Press. In recent years, the concept of "moral injury" has been increasingly deployed to refer to a particular form of injurious shame.

19. Jonathan Shay is often credited with introducing the concept of moral injury, and it has since been refined, debated, and operationalized by Shay, Brett Litz, and others. Jonathan Shay 1994. *Achilles in Vietnam: Combat trauma and the undoing of character.* New York: Scribner; Jonathan Shay 2014. Moral injury. *Psychoanalytic Psychology 31*: 182–191; Brett T. Litz, N. Stein, E. Delaney, L. Lebowitz, W. P. Nash, C. Silva, & S. Maguen 2009. Moral injury and moral repair in war veterans: A preliminary model and intervention strategy. *Clinical Psychology Review 29*: 695–706; Brett T. Litz & Patricia K. Kerig 2019. Introduction to the special issue on moral injury: Conceptual challenges, methodological issues, and clinical applications. *Journal of Traumatic Stress 32*: 341–349.

20. John Tirman 2011. *The deaths of others: The fate of civilians in America's wars.* New York: Oxford University Press; Andrew Bacevich 2016. *America's war for the Greater Middle East: A military history.* New York: Random House. For a recent collection of writings on the topic, see Robert Emmet Meagher & Douglas A. Pryer, eds., *War and moral injury: A reader.* Eugene, OR: Cascade Books.

21. Hugh Gusterson 2016. *Drone: Remote control warfare.* Cambridge, MA: MIT Press.

22. Stephanie Bonnes 2017. The bureaucratic harassment of U.S. Servicewomen. *Gender & Society 31*: 804–829, quote from p. 804.

23. Rebecca Lane, Erika Tarzi, Kristen Post, & Eric Gauldin 2018. Marine corps organizational research project report to Personnel Studies and Oversight Office: Marines' perspectives on various aspects of marine corps organizational culture, USCM Center For Advanced Operational Culture Learning, EDCOM, March 30.

24. Carrie L. Lucas, Julie A. Cederbaum, Sarah Kintzle, & Carl Andrew Castro 2019. An examination of stalking experiences during military service among female and male veterans and associations with PTSD and depression. *Journal of Interpersonal Violence 34*: 1–22.

25. Suzanne Gordon 2018. *Wounds of war: How the VA delivers health, healing, and hope to the nation's veterans.* Ithaca & London: ILR Press. See also Kristen J. Leslie 2019. Betrayal by friendly fire. Pp. 245–255 in Robert Emmet Meagher & Douglas A. Pryer, eds., *War and moral injury: A reader.* Eugene, OR: Cascade Books.

26. Randy Shilts 1993. *Conduct unbecoming: Gays and lesbians in the U.S. military.* New York: St. Martin's Press, p. 521.

27. Robert I. Correales 2008. Don't Ask, Don't Tell: A dying policy on the precipice. *Western Law Review 44*: 413–476.

28. Brandon Alford & Shawna J. Lee 2016. Toward complete inclusion: Lesbian, gay, bisexual, and transgender military service members after repeal of Don't Ask, Don't Tell. *Social Work 61*: 257–265, quote from p. 257. See also Catherine Connell 2017. Now that we can ask and tell: The social movement legacy of the DADT repeal. *Sociology Compass 11*: 1–13.

29. Sanam Naraghi Anderlini 2007. *Women building peace: What they do, why it matters.* Boulder & London: Lynne Rienner Publishers; Carol Cohn 2004. Feminist peace-making. *Women's Review of Books 21* (5): 8–9; Carol Cohn & Ruth Jacobson 2013. Women and political activism in the face of war and militarization. Pp. 102–123 in Carol Cohn, ed., *Women and wars.* Malden, MA: Polity; Gwyn Kirk 1989. Our Greenham Common: Feminism and nonviolence. Pp 115–130 in Adrienne Harris & Ynestra King, eds., *Rocking the ship of state: Toward a feminist peace politics.* Boulder, San Francisco, & London: Westview Press; Lisa Leitz 2014. *Fighting for peace: Veterans and military families in the anti-Iraq War movement.* Minneapolis: University of Minnesota Press; Rhoda Linton 1989. Seneca women's peace camp: Shapes of things to come. Pp. 239–261 in Adrienne Harris & Ynestra King, eds., *Rocking the ship of state: Toward a feminist peace politics.* Boulder, San Francisco, & London: Westview Press; Amy Swerdlow 1989. Pure milk, not poison: Women strike for peace and the Test Ban Treaty of 1963. Pp. 225–237 in Adrienne Harris & Ynestra King, eds., *Rocking the ship of state: Toward a feminist peace politics*; Lawrence S. Wittner 1969. *Rebels against war: The American peace movement, 1941–1960.* New York & London: Columbia University Press.

30. Orna Sasson-Levey, Yagil Levy, & Edna Lomsky-Feder 2011. Women breaking the silence: Military service, gender and antiwar protest. *Gender & Society 25*: 740–763. Boulder, San Francisco, & London: Westview Press. See also Rosa del Duca, 2019. *Breaking cadence: One woman's war against the war.* Portland, OR: Ooligan Press.

31. Leila J. Rupp & Verta Taylor 1987. *Survival in the doldrums: The American women's movement, 1945–the 1960s.* New York & Oxford: Oxford University Press, p. 7. See also Suzanne Staggenborg & Verta Taylor 2005. What ever happened to the women's movement? *Mobilization: An International Journal 10*: 37–52; Verta Taylor 1989. Social movement continuity: The women's movement in abeyance. *American Sociological Review 54*: 761–775.

32. Wilson. M. Powell, ed. 2008. *The democratization of Veterans For Peace, 1995–2007.* Veterans For Peace.

33. David Flores 2016. From prowar soldier to antiwar activist: Change and continuity in the narratives of political conversion among Iraq War Veterans. *Symbolic Interaction* (1533-8665 online); Matthew Gutmann & Catherine Lutz 2010. *Breaking ranks: Iraq veterans speak out against the war.* Berkeley: University of California Press; Jonathan W. Hutto 2008. *Antiwar soldier: How to dissent within the ranks of the military.* New York: Nation Books; Leitz, 2014.

34. Patricia Hill Collins 1990. *Black feminist thought: Knowledge, consciousness and the politics of empowerment.* New York: Routledge.

35. Karl Marx 1988 (1844). *Economic and philosophic manuscripts of 1844.* Buffalo, NY: Prometheus Books.

36. Freire argued that traditional literacy projects in peasant communities were bound to fail, based as they were on what he called "banking education," top-down methods that assumed educators had knowledge that they deposited into the heads of learners. Instead, Freire insisted on "dialogical" education grounded in the existing situated knowledge of peasants. Through critical dialogue, he argued, people simultaneously

learned to read, while collectively de-coding the social relations around them, and acting to take control of their lives. Paulo Freire 1970. *Pedagogy of the oppressed*. New York: Herder & Herder.

37. Dorothy E. Smith 1989. *The everyday world as problematic: A feminist sociology*. Boston: Northeastern University Press.

38. Joan Acker 2006. Inequality regimes: Gender, class, and race in organizations. *Gender & Society 20*: 441–464.

39. Robin DiAngelo 2018. *White fragility: Why it's so hard for White people to talk about racism*. Boston: Beacon Press, pp. 27, 51.

40. Kimberle Williams Crenshaw 1989. Demarginalizing the intersection of race and sex: A Black feminist critique of antidiscrimination doctrine, feminist theory and antiracist politics. *University of Chicago Legal Forum 140*: 139–167; Kimberle Williams Crenshaw 1991. Mapping the margins: Intersectionality, identity politics and violence against women of color. *Stanford Law Review 43*: 1241–1299.

41. Hancock, 2016. Black women's contributions have always been central to the development of intersectionality. Combahee River Collective 1977. A Black feminist statement. Pp. 13–22 in Gloria Hull & Patricia Bell Scott, eds., *All the women are White, all the Blacks are men, but some of us are brave: Black women's studies*. New York: Feminist Press. A generation of women of color have broadened and deepened the field over the years, for instance in my field of sociology see: Maxine Baca Zinn & Bonnie Thornton Dill 1996. Theorizing difference from multiracial feminism. *Feminist Studies 22*: 321–331; Maxine Baca Zinn & Ruth Enid Zambrana 2019. Chicanas/Latinas advance intersectional thought and practice. *Gender & Society 33*: 677–702; Bonnie Thornton Dill & Ruth Enid Zambrana 2009. *Emerging intersections: Race, class, and gender in theory, policy, and practice*. New Brunswick, NJ: Rutgers University Press; Evelyn Nakano Glenn 2009. *Unequal freedoms: How race and gender shaped American citizenship*. Cambridge, MA: Harvard University Press; Joya Misra 2018. Categories, structures, and intersectional theory. Pp. 111–130 in James W. Messerschmidt, Patricia Yancey Martin, Michael A. Messner & Raewyn Connell, eds., *Gender reckonings: New social theory and research*. New York: New York University Press; Mignon R. Moore 2012. Intersectionality and the study of Black, sexual minority women. *Gender & Society 26*: 33–39.

42. Audre Lorde 2007 (1984). Age, race, class, and sex: Women redefining difference. Pp. 114–123 in Audre Lorde, *Sister outsider: Essays and speeches*. Berkeley: Crossing Press, p. 14.

43. Sociologist Katarzyna Wojnicka argues that "intersectionality sheds a new light on social movements and stratification in two regards: First, regarding the composition of movements—in terms of its diversity, or the lack of it. It makes visible internal struggles about identities and categories as well as (unintended) mechanisms of exclusion. Secondly, it reveals intersectionality as a political strategy. Creating narratives of the very marginalised and making multiple dimensions of their exploitation and discrimination visible helps to produce alternative knowledge, challenging dominate frames within society and creating more opportunities to challenge unequal power structures." Katarzyna Wojnicka 2019. Social movements and intersectionality: The

case of migrants' social activism. Pp. 168–184 in S. Zajak & S. Haunss, eds., *Social stratification and social movements*. London: Routledge. See also Hajir Yazdiha 2020. An intersectional theory of strategic action: Socially located memories, cultural knowledge, and Muslim rights. *Mobilization: An International Journal 25*: 475–492.

44. Patricia Hill Collins 2019. *Intersectionality as critical social theory*. Durham & London: Duke University Press, p. 146.

45. Barbara Omolade 1989. We speak for the planet. Pp. 171–189 in Adrienne Harris & Ynestra King, eds., *Rocking the ship of state: Toward a feminist peace politics*. Boulder, San Francisco, & London: Westview Press, p. 172.

46. Millennials, most often defined as those Americans born between 1981 and 1996, are substantially more racially diverse than earlier generations of Americans, and this is an important factor for the ways that they are now viewing and acting in progressive social movements. But scholar Joseph Cabosky warns against simplistic overgeneralizations about the 70 million people of this generation who are also diverse geographically, economically, and educationally. Sixty percent of millennials "lean Democratic" politically, Cabosky notes, but we should be cautious about predicting that they will move the nation in radically progressive ways. Joseph Cabosky 2019. If you're using "Millennial" as a meaningful measurement, you should probably stop. *The Conversation*, October 22.

47. Ruth Milkman 2014. Millennial movements: Occupy Wall Street and the Dreamers. *Dissent 61* (3): 55–59; Ruth Milkman 2017. "A new political generation: Millennials and the post-2008 wave of protest. *American Sociological Review 82* (1): 1–31; Jo Reger 2019. The making of a march: Identity, intersectionality and diffusion of U.S. feminism. Pp. 2–22 in Jo Reger, ed., *Nevertheless, they persisted: Feminisms and continued resistance in the U.S. women's movement*. New York & London: Routledge.

48. Veronica Terriquez 2015. Intersectional mobilization, social movement spillover, and queer youth leadership in the immigrant rights movement. *Social Problems 62* (3): 343–362. See also Veronica Terriquez 2015. Training young activists: Grassroots organizing and youths' civic and political trajectories. *Sociological Perspectives 58*: 223–242; C. Shawn McGuffey 2018. Intersectionality, cognition, disclosure and black LGBT views on civil rights and marriage equality. *Du Bois Review 15*: 441–465; Heather Hurwitz McKee 2019. #FemGA #SayHerName #NotHereForBoys: Feminist spillover in U.S. social movements, 2011-2016. Pp 115–132 in Jo Reger, ed. *Nevertheless, they persisted: Feminisms and continued resistance in the U.S. women's movement*. New York and London: Routledge; Meyer, David S. and Nancy Whittier 1994. "Social Movement Spillover." *Social Problems 41*(2): 277; Fatima Suarez 2019. Identifying with inclusivity: Intersectional Chicana feminisms. Pp. 25–42 in Jo Reger, ed. *Nevertheless, they persisted: Feminisms and continued resistance in the U.S. women's movement*. New York and London: Routledge.

49. Hurwitz, 2019, p. 123.

50. Reger, 2019, p. 13.

51. Collins, 1990.

52. Suarez, 2019, p. 25.

53. I don't want to speculate too deeply based on my limited observations, but I wonder if the apparent centering of intersectionality in the 2020 march was linked to the decline of "pussy hats." In examining the dearth of intersectionality in earlier feminist "Slutwalks," sociologist Theresa Allen Hunt argues that White organizers' lack of understanding of how gendered racism impacts women of color created a blind-spot that limited the impact of these anti-rape protests. Theresa Ann Hunt 2018. A movement divided: Slutwalks, protest repertoires and the privilege of nudity. *Social Movements Studies* 17: 541–557.

54. Charlene A. Carruthers argues that progressive social movement work should proceed through a "Black queer feminist lens," which she views as "a political praxis (practice and theory) based on Black feminist and LGBTQ traditions and knowledge, through which people and groups see to bring their full selves into the process of dismantling all systems of oppression." Charlene A. Carruthers 2018. *Unapologetic: A Black, queer, and feminist mandate for radical movements.* Boston: Beacon Press, p. 10. See also Ronni Michelle Greenwood 2008. Intersectional political consciousness: Appreciation for intergroup differences and solidarity in diverse groups. *Psychology of Women Quarterly 32*: 36–47; Zakiya Luna 2016. "Truly a women of color organization": Negotiating sameness and difference in the pursuit of intersectionality. *Gender & Society 30*: 769–790.

55. Michael Messner 2019. *Guys like me: Five wars, five veterans for peace.* New Brunswick, NJ: Rutgers University Press.

56. Maxine Baca Zinn, Lynn Weber Cannon, Elizabeth Higgenbotham, & Bonnie Thornton Dill 1986. The costs of exclusionary practices in women's studies. *Signs: Journal of Women in Culture and Society 11*: 290–303.

57. Robin Morgan, ed. 1970. *Sisterhood is powerful: An anthology of writings from the women's liberation movement.* New York: Vintage Books.

58. My colleagues and I develop this analogy between "patchwork quilt" vs. "prism of difference" orientations to inclusiveness in the Introduction to our edited book. Maxine Baca Zinn, Pierrette Hondagneu-Sotelo, Michael A. Messner, & Stephanie Nawyn, eds. 2020. *Gender through the prism of difference* (6th ed.). New York & Oxford: Oxford University Press.

59. Greenwood, 2008, p. 36.

60. In *Some Men*, a book on men's work in gender-based violence prevention movements, my co-authors Max Greenberg, Tal Peretz, and I introduced the idea of "organic intersectionality," based on our observations of the ways that antiviolence activists who came from working-class, Black, Latino, and queer backgrounds brought situated knowledge of race, class, and sexual oppression to the work, deepening and broadening what had become a highly professionalized, marketized, and depoliticized field of action that focused narrowly on measurable outcomes in gender-based violence prevention. Michael A. Messner, Max A. Greenberg, & Tal Peretz 2015. *Some men: Feminist allies and the movement to end violence against women.* New York: Oxford University Press.

61. The idea to include short interludes between chapters came to me from reading and teaching one of my favorite books: Ann Arnett Ferguson 2000. *Bad boys: Public schools and the making of Black masculinity.* Ann Arbor: University of Michigan Press.

Chapter 2

1. Michael A. Messner 2019. *Guys like me: Five wars, five veterans for peace*. New Brunswick, NJ: Rutgers University Press.
2. The film *The Great Santini* is based on the novel of the same title, written in 1976 by Pat Conroy. Some of Conroy's other books also offer glimpses into the cruelty of the rigidly masculine culture of the military and military schools. Pat Conroy 1976. *The great Santini*. New York: Random House; Pat Conroy 1980. *The lords of discipline*. New York: Houghton Mifflin.
3. Catherine Lutz 2004. Living room terrorists: Rates of domestic violence are three to five times higher among military couples than among civilian ones. *Women's Review of Books* 21 (5): 17–18, quote from p. 17. Monisha Ríos 2019. The glue is still drying. Pp. 83–94 in Robert Emmet Meagher and Douglas A. Pryer, eds., *War and moral injury: A reader*. Eugene, OR: Cascade Books.
4. Brenda L. Moore noted in 1996 that following the 1973 shift to all-volunteer force, "the number women on active duty increased threefold from 1973–1979; the number of African American women increased fivefold," and this rapid increase continued into the 1980s and 1990s. Brenda L. Moore 1996. From underrepresentation to over-representation: African American women. Pp. 115–135 in Judith Hicks Stiehm, ed., *It's our military too! Women and the U.S. military*. Philadelphia: Temple University Press, pp. 123–124.
5. In 2005, the year Wendy Barranco arrived in Tikrit, more than 800 U.S. troops were killed in the Iraq War, and roughly 5,500 were wounded. As is usually the case in times of war, things were even worse for civilians on the ground; roughly 16,500 Iraqi civilians perished that year. As Barranco left Iraq in mid-2006, the war was growing even more deadly. That year, the civilian body count nearly doubled to 29,500. https://www.iraqbodycount.org/. John Tirman argues that official numbers of civilian war deaths in Iraq and Afghanistan are likely lower than the true death count. John Tirman 2011. *The deaths of others: The fate of civilians in America's wars*. New York: Oxford University Press, p. 317.
6. Phoenix Johnson identifies as a gender non-binary Native Two-Spirit person, who prefers gender-neutral pronouns, which I deploy throughout the book when discussing them.
7. For an overview of the historical and contemporary price paid by Native peoples and Native lands for U.S. militarization, see Winona LaDuke, with Sean Aaron Cruz 2012. *The militarization of Indian country*. East Lansing: Makwa Enewed.
8. Please see note 4 in Chapter 1 for some background on Native American Two-Spirit people.
9. Monique Salhab identifies as a queer gender non-binary woman, who prefers gender-neutral pronouns, which I deploy throughout the book when discussing them.
10. A documentary film about LGBTQ veterans was entitled "The Camouflage Closet." http://www.camouflagecloset.com.
11. Psychologists for Social Responsibility works "to advance peace and social justice through the ethical use of psychological knowledge, research, and practice." (https://

psysr.net). An article in the journal sponsored by PsySR criticizes the past and current conventional uses of professional psychology to promote militarism: Mark Pilisuk & Ines-Lena Mahr 2015. Psychology and the prevention of war trauma. *Journal for Social Action in Counseling and Psychology 7*: 122–142.

12. The organization's website states that "Courage to Resist supports the troops who refuse to fight, or who face consequences for acting on conscience, in opposition to illegal wars, occupations, the policies of empire abroad and martial law at home." https://couragetoresist.org.

13. DeBarros's four-minute speech can be viewed here: https://www.facebook.com/watch/?v=2179645452052168.

14. Brittany Ramos DeBarros 2014. Four things you may not know about veterans. *Living Cities*, November 11. https://www.livingcities.org/blog/719-four-things-you-may-not-know-about-veterans; Brittany Ramos DeBarros 2015. One female veteran's experience: And other #Goodreads about the state of America's veterans. *Living Cities*, November 13. https://www.livingcities.org/blog/986-one-female-veteran-s-experience-and-other-goodreads-about-the-state-of-america-s-veterans.

15. Research shows that women deployed to Iraq and Afghanistan share with their male colleagues the risk of PTSD following combat exposure, but women also face a high risk of sexual assault and sexual harassment. Stephanie Bonnes 2017. The bureaucratic harassment of U.S. servicewomen. *Gender & Society 31*: 804–829; Amy E. Street, Dwayne Vogt, & Lissa Dutra 2009. A new generation of women veterans: Stressors faced by women deployed to Iraq and Afghanistan. *Clinical Psychology Review 29*: 685–694.

16. Angela Y. Davis 2016. *Freedom is a constant struggle: Ferguson, Palestine, and the foundations of a movement*. Chicago: Haymarket Books.

Interlude 2

1. Michael A. Messner 2005. The triad of violence in men's sports. In E. Buchwald, P. R. Fletcher, & M. Roth, eds. *Transforming a rape culture*. Minneapolis: Milkweed Editions; Michael A. Messner 2014. Can locker room rape culture be prevented? *Contexts: Understanding People in Their Social Worlds* (Spring); Michael A. Messner 2016. Bad men, good men, bystanders: Who is the rapist? *Gender & Society 30*: 57–66.

Chapter 3

1. Charlene A. Carruthers 2018. *Unapologetic: A Black, queer, and feminist mandate for radical movements*. Boston: Beacon Press, p. 3.

2. There is a rich social-scientific literature on the ways that organizations are structured by race, class, and gender in ways that systematically reinforce class privileges,

and privileges for men, and for white people. For foundational works, see Joan Acker 1990. Hierarchies, jobs, bodies: A theory of gendered organizations. *Gender & Society* 4: 139–158; Joan Acker 2006. Inequality regimes: Gender, class, and race in organizations. *Gender & Society 20*: 441–464; Adia Harvey Wingfield 2007. The modern mammy and the angry Black man: African-American professionals' experiences with gendered racism in the workplace. *Race, Gender and Class 14*: 196–212.

3. Rosabeth Moss Kanter 1977. *Men and women of the corporation.* New York: Basic.

4. Wingfield, 2007; Adia Harvey Wingfield 2010. Are some emotions marked "White only"? Racialized feeling rules in professional workplaces. *Social Problems 57: 251–266*; Wingfield, Adia Harvey, & Renee Skeete 2014. Maintaining hierarchies in predominantly White organizations: A theory of racial tasks. *American Behavioral Scientist 58*: 274–287.

5. Veterans For Peace 2016. Board Candidates. https://www.veteransforpeace.org/who-we-are/board-of-directors-new/2014-board-candidates-2

6. Sociologist Stephanie Bonnes argues that servicewomen with combat experience "are able to gain inclusion as military insiders because they can access" what sociologist Raewyn Connell calls "patriarchal dividends." Stephanie Bonnes 2020. Servicewomen's responses to sexual harassment: The importance of identity work and masculinity in a gendered organization. *Violence Against Women 26*: 1656–1680.

7. My co-author Tal Peretz coined the term "the pedestal effect." See Michael A. Messner, Max A. Greenberg, & Tal Peretz 2015. *Some men: Feminist allies and the movement to end violence against women.* New York: Oxford University Press.

8. Sociologists James Jasper, Michael Young, and Elke Zuern, in their sweeping study of the social construction of political "heroes, villains, victims and minions" argue that "in war, heroism is especially gendered," noting how in the buildup to the Spanish-American War "[m]anhood was the great symbol of strength, and men who opposed the war could be portrayed as wearing petticoats and being overly influenced by suffragists." This association of men with heroic military heroism, ironically, still tends to inflect leadership in veterans' peace organizations. James M. Jasper, Michael P. Young, & Elke Zuern 2020. *Public characters: The politics of reputation and blame.* New York: Oxford University Press.

9. I use the term "microaggressions" here because it is widely used, and especially because some of my interviewees use the term to describe their experiences. However, some racial justice activists and writers, such as Ibram X. Kendi, have criticized the use of "microaggression," due to the ways it may psychologize and depoliticize "racist abuse" in this "so-called post-racial era." Ibram X. Kendi 2019. *How to be an antiracist.* New York: One World, pp. 46–47.

10. Kevin L. Nadal, Katie E. Griffin, Yinglee Wong, Sahran Hamit, & Morgan Rasmus 2014. The impact of racial microaggressions on mental health: Counseling implications for clients of color. *Journal of Counseling and Development 92*: 57–66. Research points to similar troubles for highly educated academic faculty of color. See Ruth Enid Zambrana 2018. *Toxic ivory towers: The consequences of work stress on underrepresented minority faculty.* New Brunswick, NJ: Rutgers University Press.

11. Melissa L. Walls, John Gonzalez, Tanya Gladney, & Emily Onello 2015. Unconscious biases: Racial microaggressions in American Indian healthcare. *Journal of the American Board of Family Medicine 28*: 231–239.
12. Kimberly F. Balsam, Yamile Molina, Blair Beadnell, Jane Simoni & Karina Walters 2014. Measuring multiple minority stress: The LGBT people of color microaggressions scale. *Cultural Diversity and Ethnic Minority Psychology 17*: 163–174.
13. Paige L. Sweet 2019. The sociology of gaslighting. *American Sociological Review 84*: 851–875.
14. Peter Lyman 1981. The politics of anger: On silence, ressentiment, and political speech." *Socialist Review 57*: 55–74.
15. Audre Lorde 1981. The uses of anger: Women responding to racism. Keynote address, National Women's Studies Association, Storrs, CT, June. https://www.blackpast.org/african-american-history/speeches-african-american-history/1981-audre-lorde-uses-anger-women-responding-racism/
16. James M. Jasper 2018. *The emotions of protest*. Chicago & London: University of Chicago Press, p. 7.
17. Groves noted that men constituted only about 20% of animal rights activists, but "[a]ctivists praised men's anger, but I never heard them praise a woman's ... Men's willingness to express their feelings was considered a sign of fearlessness, but in women in was a sign of weakness." Julian McAllister Groves 1997. *Hearts and minds: The controversy over laboratory animals*. Philadelphia: Temple University Press.
18. Verta Taylor 1996. *Rock-a-by baby: Feminism, self-help, and postpartum depression*. New York: Routledge; Verta Taylor & Leila J. Rupp 2002. Loving internationalism: The emotion culture of transnational women's organizations, 1888–1945. *Mobilization 7*: 125–144.
19. Carrie L. Lucas, Julie A. Cederbaum, Sarah Kintzle, & Carl Andrew Castro 2019. An examination of stalking experiences during military service among female and male veterans and associations with PTSD and depression. *Journal of Interpersonal Violence*, pp. 1–22
20. Cynthia Enloe 2004. *The curious feminist: Searching for women in a new age of empire*. Berkeley: University of California Press, p. 154.
21. Cecilia Taska, Mariangela Rapetti, Mauro Giovanni Cara, & Binca Fadda 2012. Women and hysteria in the history of mental health. *Clinical Practice & Epidemiology in Mental Health 8*: 110–119, quote from p. 110. See also Barbara Ehrenreich & Dierdre English 2005 (1978). *For her own good: Two centuries of experts' advice to women*. New York: Anchor Books. Barbara Ehrenreich & Dierdre English 2010. *Witches, midwives and nurses: A history of women healers* (2nd ed.). New York: The Feminist Press at CUNY.
22. George L. Mosse 2000. Shell shock as a social disease. *Journal of Contemporary History 35*: 101–108, pp. 103–104
23. Wingfield, 2010.
24. Catrice M. Jackson 2017. *White spaces missing faces: Why women of color don't trust white women*. Omaha, NE: Catriciology Enterprises.

25. Robin DiAngelo 2018. *White fragility: Why it's so hard for white people to talk about racism.* Boston: Beacon Press, p. 134.

26. DiAngelo, 2018, p. 134.

27. This short letter and its accompanying graphic is worth reading as a succinct overview of systemic processes of gendered racism, faced by women of color in progressive organizations. Brittany Ramos DeBarros 2019. An open letter on the systemic mistreatment of womxn of color in social justice spaces. *Time's Up Common Defense* (February 5). https://medium.com/timesupprogressives/ times-up-common-defense-3a0e0795cf0d.

28. William J. Goode 1980. Why men resist. *Dissent* (Spring).

Interlude 3

1. I lightly edited this six-minute podcast interview for clarity and brevity. The full podcast can be found here: https://www.sfreporter.com/podcasts/podcast/ 2020/06/05/covid-19-response-the-heavy-lifet/?eType=EmailBlastContent&eId =31c8ff2b-cad1-4710-bf24-f801d75704f1

Chapter 4

1. *La Posada sin Fronteras* translates to English as "the inn without borders," a progressive adaptation of common pre-Christmas *Posada* rituals among Roman Catholics.

2. Pierrette Hondagneu-Sotelo 2008. *God's heart has no borders: How religious activists are working for immigrant rights.* Berkeley: University of California Press. See also Pierrette Hondagneu-Sotelo, Genelle Gaudinez, Hector Lara & Billie C. Ortiz 2004. "There's a spirit that transcends the border": Faith, ritual, and postnational protest at the U.S.-Mexico Border. *Sociological perspectives 47*: 133–159.

3. During the ten months between their arrest and acquittal, DeBarros and Barranco used their case as a platform from which to speak and write about migrant justice. See, for instance, Wendy Barranco 2019. Colonizers hold the keys to the cages and the camps: Veterans and clergy put the government on trial. *Medium*, October 28.

4. These ongoing efforts reflect the membership's radical understandings, that war and militarism are connected with racial injustice, environmental degradation, nationalism, and colonialism. These coalitional efforts can sometimes be seen as classic "abeyance strategies" by movement organizations that, by themselves, are momentarily too small for stand-alone efforts and actions. For example, the VFP chapter with whom I have worked as a participant observer for the past four years in Santa Fe, NM, has perhaps 90 members on paper, but fewer than ten normally show up for monthly chapter meetings. The chapter's longstanding peace vigil on a busy street corner continues every Friday at noon. But on any given week, there may be only a half-dozen,

perhaps as few as three or four members waving VFP banners to honking cars. By contrast, the chapter actively supports and has a visible presence in other local political efforts.

5. Some Marxist organizations' focus on class oppression as the principle historical contradiction to be overcome—followed presumably by equality for women and for racial minorities "after the revolution"—is a prime example of movement reductionism. There are many other examples, including the White, middle-class focus of much of the 1960s women's movement; the male domination of much of the Black Power movement of that same era; the male and White middle-class basis and bias of the early 1970s and 1980s gay and lesbian rights movement, etc. Intersectionality, as I discussed in Chapter 1, promotes an analysis that illuminates the oppressive limits of singular-identity-based movements, and also points to strategic actions that aim to address multiple forms of oppression without a priori privileging one over others.

6. James M. Jasper 2004. A strategic approach to collective action: Looking for agency in social movement choices. *Mobilization: An International Journal 9*: 1–16, quote from p. 7.

7. Arlington West is a high-profile effort, initiated shortly after the U.S. invasions of Afghanistan and Iraq, by the Santa Barbara, California, and Santa Monica, California, chapters of Veterans For Peace. For many years, each Sunday at those location and also in San Diego and occasionally other locations, VFP members line up row after row of white crosses on the beach, each to commemorate a U.S. soldier killed in the Middle East wars. Arlington West is an emotionally arresting visual display that captures the growing numbers of casualties in ongoing wars, while zeroing in on the human face of each individual killed soldier. Still now, every Sunday the Santa Monica VFP members set this up at sunrise, and take it down at sunset, and during the daylight hours a group of them sits behind a table full of VFP and other anti-war literature, always ready to engage with passers-by. They told me that they have never kept a count, but they guess that over the years they have spoken with "tens of thousands" of American citizens and international visitors about war and peace. For photos, video clips and other information on Arlington West, see: http://www.arlingtonwestsantamonica.org/contact.html.

8. Sarah Parvini 2020. To reform or reconstruct? Young Black activists, challenging "respectability politics" of their elders, give voice to a new movement for social change. *Los Angeles Times*, June 15.

9. Speaking simultaneously to the intersectional connections that younger, progressive activists commonly make today, and to the salience of race—particularly Blackness, in this moment—a Black lesbian marcher told an *LA Times* reporter that it was rare for her to be able to publicly express all parts of her identity. "You have to put your Blackness first," she said. "My lesbianism, that comes later. Being Black and a woman in America, it is really tough." Hailey Branson-Potts & Matt Stiles 2020. Thousands take to the streets for All Black Lives Matter rally. *Los Angeles Times*, June 15.

10. About Face: Veterans Against the War 2020. TROOPS: Stand down for Black Lives. *Medium.com*, May 29.

11. Trayvon Martin, a 17-year-old Black youth in Sanford, Florida, was shot and killed in 2012 by George Zimmerman, a neighborhood watch coordinator. Zimmerman pled self-defense and was found not guilty of murder in 2013. Peaceful protests and vigils were held in over 100 U.S. cities in the aftermath of the verdict.

12. Alex Heitt 2019. Albuquerque Proud Boys demonstration generates resistance. *DailyLobo.com*, September 16; Alex Reichbach 2019. Alt-right groups rally, outnumbered by counterprotestors. *NMPoliticalReport*, September 15.

13. Tom Nolan 2020. Militarization has fostered a policing culture that sets up protestors as "the enemy." *The Conversation*, June 2. For a book-length critical analysis of this topic, see Radley Balco 2014. *Rise of the warrior cop: The militarization of America's police forces*. New York: Public Affairs.

14. Patricia Hill Collins 1986. Learning from the outsider within: The sociological significance of Black feminist thought. *Social Problems 33*: 14–32.

15. Cherrie Moraga & Anzaldua, Gloria 1981. *This bridge called my back: Writings by radical women of color*. Watertown, MA: Persephone Press.

16. In 1979, Michelle Wallace penned a controversial and scathing critique of the sexism of some men leaders of the Black Power movement. Michelle Wallace 1979. *Black macho and the myth of the super-woman*. New York: Warner Books. The book was widely debated and criticized. See, for instance, the pushback from a key Black male sociologist of the time: Robert Staples 1979. The myth of the Black macho: A response to angry Black feminists. *The Black Scholar 10*.

17. "Make Drag, Not War" still maintains a colorful and lively website: https://www.veteranartists.org/make-drag-not-war/.

18. In 2011, this group generated "Service: When women come marching home," a documentary film, by Marcia Rock and Patricia Lee Stotter, focusing on the experiences of post-9/11 women veterans returning from the U.S. War in Afghanistan.

19. Christopher Mele 2016. Veterans to serve as "human shields" for Dakota Access Pipeline protestors, *The New York Times*, December 14.

20. Sarah van Gelder 2016. Veteran Wesley Clark Jr: Why I knelt before Standing Rock elders and asked for forgiveness. *YES! Magazine*, December 22.

21. For critical investigative reporting on Clark's and Wood's management of the funds raised for *Veterans Stand*, see Paige Blankenbuehler 2018. Cashing in on Standing Rock: How *Veterans Stand* squandered $1.4 million raised around the #NoDAPL. *HighCountryNews*, April 13.

22. Stephen W. Silliman 2008. The "Old West" in the Middle East: U.S. military metaphors in real and imagined Indian country. *American Anthropologist 110*: 237–247.

23. Winona LaDuke with Sean Aaron Cruz 2012. *The militarization of Indian country.* East Lansing: Makwa Enewed, p. 9.

24. Liz Fields 2016. Veterans brought cameras, but also "complete chaos" to Standing Rock. *Vice News*, December 9.

25. Jeffrey Montez de Oca 2012. White domestic goddess on a postmodern plantation: Charity and commodity racism in *The Blind Side*. *Sociology of Sport Journal 29*: 131–151.

26. Estes argues that during the Standing Rock opposition, "While the media foregrounded images of the camp's leadership, often donning headdresses, and frequently men, it was common for Two-Spirited people and women to hold leadership roles in all aspects of camp life." Nick Estes 2019. *Our history is the future: Standing Rock versus the Dakota Access Pipeline, and the long tradition of Indigenous resistance.* London & New York: Verso, p. 62.

27. In her powerful book about women in Okinawa, Akemi Johnson points out that 70% of U.S. bases in Japan are "still crowded in tiny Okinawa, mostly in the main island. They add 50,000 American military personnel, civilian contractors, and family members to the island's population of 1.4 million . . . in past years Okinawa depended on the bases for jobs and other income. Today though, the U.S. military presence accounts for only 5% of the local economy. Many argue that the closure of the bases would give way to greater economic development . . ." The U.S. military presence in Okinawa is riddled with decades of sexual exploitation and violence against local women, though Johnson deftly probes local women's mixed, often ambivalent relationships with U.S. military men. Akemi Johnson 2019. *Night in the American village: Women in the shadow of U.S. military bases in Okinawa.* New York & London: The New Press, pp. 4–5.

28. Corrie Grosse 2019. Ecofeminism and climate justice. Pp. 185–203 in Jo Reger, ed., *Nevertheless, they persisted: Feminisms and continued resistance in the U.S. women's movement.* New York & London: Routledge, p. 186.

29. Eve Tuck & K. Wayne Yang 2012. Decolonization is not a metaphor. *Decolonization: Indigeneity, Education & Society 1*: 1–40, quote from p. 2.

30. The "VFP Global Warming Response Resolution" passed 566–13 at the 2019 business meeting in Spokane. See the full resolution here: https://www.veteransforpeace.org/2019ballot/2019-01.

31. Medea Benjamin 2019. Ten ways that the climate crisis and militarization are intertwined. *Foreign policy in focus*, September 27. See also Oliver Belcher, Patrick Bigger, Ben Neimark, & Cara Kennelly 2019. Hidden carbon costs of the "everywhere war": Logistics, geopolitical ecology, and the carbon boot-print of the US military. *Transactions of the Institute of British Geographers*, 1–16.

32. https://www.sdvfp.org/resources/climate-change/.

33. https://www.yuccanm.org/who-we-are.

34. Brian Ward 2020. From the Green New Deal to the Red Deal. *The Red Nation*, April 10. https://therednation.org/2020/04/10/from-the-green-new-deal-to-the-red-deal/.

35. The relationship between conventional intersectional social justice activism and decolonial struggles by Indigenous peoples is complicated. Sociologist Jeffrey Montez de Oca (private correspondence) wrote that when joining progressive coalitions, Native Tribes' calls for "decolonization" means, "more than anything else, calling for a conscious recognition of settler colonialism and Indigenous peoples in social justice movements. [This] draws attention to the fact that dominant social justice frameworks can be colonial in their moves to liberation. If we want to engage in intersectional analyses then we cannot view race and imperialism or social justice in

narrow terms. We also need to understand that decolonization requires dismantling colonizing nation-states, their institutions and ways of thinking."

36. LaDuke with Cruz, 2012, p. 37.

37. Kai Bird & Martin J. Sherwin 2006. *American Prometheus: The triumph and tragedy of J. Robert Oppenheimer.* New York: Vintage Books.

38. At the national VFP convention in Spokane, Washington, in 2019, a local Indigenous leader addressed the convention and spoke of the cancer epidemic among Native uranium miners as "the new smallpox," referencing the genocidal (and some say, purposive) infection of Indigenous peoples with smallpox by White settlers in the 18th Century.

39. Tina Cordova 2018. Tularosa Basin Downwinders. *Atomic Heritage Foundation*, July 31. https://www.atomicheritage.org/history/tularosa-basin-downwinders.

Chapter 5

1. Here, I supply short edited excerpts from DeBarros's speech, which can be viewed in its entirety here: https://www.facebook.com/veteransforpeace/videos/903193573380502

2. Leila J. Rupp & Verta Taylor 1987. *Survival in the doldrums: The American women's movement, 1945–the 1960s.* New York & Oxford: Oxford University Press. Verta Taylor 1989. Social movement continuity: The women's movement in abeyance. *American Sociological Review 54*: 761–775.

3. bell hooks 1984. *Feminist theory: From margin to center.* Boston: South End Press.

4. Benita Roth 2010. *Separate roads to feminism: Black, Chicana, and White feminist movements in America's second wave.* Cambridge: Cambridge University Press, p. 8.

5. Dana R. Fisher 2019. *American resistance: From the Women's March to the Blue Wave.* New York: Columbia University Press, pp. 6, 16–17.

6. Ange-Marie Hancock 2016. *Intersectionality: An intellectual history.* New York: Oxford University Press, p. 4.

7. Wendy Barranco is an exception to this, as I first interviewed her for my previous book in November of 2017, and then followed up with interviews for this book in January and May of 2020.

8. Some lesbian feminists in the 1960s and 1970s quit the mainstream movement to form their own separate lesbian feminist organizations and communities. In her definitive history of radical feminism in the United States, historian Alice Echols traces this and other schisms and debates within the movement. Alice Echols 2019 (1989) *Daring to be bad: Radical feminism in America, 1967–1975.* Minneapolis: University of Minnesota Press. During roughly the same time period, many Black women and other women of color left the women's movement due to its White and middle-class basis and bias, some eschewing the "feminist" label and eventually adopting "womanist," a term introduced by Alice Walker. Alice Walker 1979. Coming apart. Pp. 41–53 in Alice Walker, ed., *You can't keep a good woman down: Short stories.* Orlando: Harcourt, Inc.

9. *The Golden Rule* was originally launched in 1958 as a part of a project to stop atmospheric nuclear testing. The VFP web page notes, "The restored *Golden Rule* is voyaging once more, to show that a nuclear peace is possible, and that bravery and tenacity can overcome militarism." http://www.vfpgoldenruleproject.org

10. For an historical background of this, see Cesar J. Ayala & Jose L. Bolivar 2011. *Battleship Vieques: Puerto Rico from World War II to the Korean War.* Princeton, NJ: Markus Wiener Publications.

11. For brevity, I have edited parts of this fundraising e-mail message from DeBarros and About Face.

12. Taylor, 1989.

13. Alison Dahl Crossley 2019. Online feminism is just feminism: Offline and online movement persistence. Pp. 60–78 in Jo Reger, ed., *Nevertheless, they persisted: Feminisms and continued resistance in the U.S. women's movement.* New York & London: Routledge.

References

About Face: Veterans Against the War 2020. TROOPS: Stand down for Black Lives. *Medium.com*, May 29.

Acker, Joan 1990. Hierarchies, jobs, bodies: A theory of gendered organizations. *Gender & Society 4*: 139–158.

Acker, Joan 2006. Inequality regimes: Gender, class, and race in organizations. *Gender & Society 20*: 441–464.

Alford, Brandon & Shawna J. Lee 2016. Toward complete inclusion: Lesbian, gay, bisexual, and transgender military service members after repeal of Don't Ask, Don't Tell. *Social Work 61*: 257–265.

Anderlini, Sanam Naraghi 2007. *Women building peace: What they do, why it matters.* Boulder & London: Lynne Rienner Publishers.

Ayala, Cesar J. & Jose L. Bolivar 2011. *Battleship Vieques: Puerto Rico from World War II to the Korean War*. Princeton, NJ: Markus Wiener Publications.

Baca Zinn, Maxine, Lynn Weber Cannon, Elizabeth Higgenbotham, & Bonnie Thornton Dill 1986. The costs of exclusionary practices in women's studies. *Signs: Journal of Women in Culture and Society 11*: 290–303.

Baca Zinn, Maxine & Bonnie Thornton Dill 1996. Theorizing difference from multiracial feminism. *Feminist Studies 22*: 321–331.

Baca Zinn, Maxine, Pierrette Hondagneu-Sotelo, Michael A. Messner, & Stephanie Nawyn, eds. 2020. *Gender through the prism of difference* (6th ed.). New York & Oxford: Oxford University Press.

Baca Zinn, Maxine & Ruth Enid Zambrana 2019. Chicanas/Latinas advance intersectional thought and practice. *Gender & Society 33*: 677–702.

Bacevich, Andrew 2016. *America's war for the Greater Middle East: A military history.* New York: Random House.

Balco, Radley 2014. *Rise of the warrior cop: The militarization of America's police forces.* New York: Public Affairs.

Balsam, Kimberly F., Yamile Molina, Blair Beadnell, Jane Simoni, & Karina Walters 2014. Measuring multiple minority stress: The LGBT people of color microaggressions scale. *Cultural Diversity and Ethnic Minority Psychology 17*: 163–174.

Barranco, Wendy 2019. Colonizers hold the keys to the cages and the camps: Veterans and clergy put the government on trial. *Medium*, October 28.

Belcher, Oliver, Patrick Bigger, Ben Neimark, & Cara Kennelly 2020. Hidden carbon costs of the "everywhere war": Logistics, geopolitical ecology, and the carbon boot-print of the US military. *Transactions of the Institute of British Geographers 20*: 65–80.

Beneria, Lourdes & Rebecca Blank 1989. Women and the economics of military spending. Pp 191–203 in Adrienne Harris & Ynestra King, eds., *Rocking the ship of state: Toward a feminist peace politics*. Boulder, San Francisco, & London: Westview Press.

Benjamin, Medea 2019. Ten ways that the climate crisis and militarization are intertwined. *Foreign policy in focus*, September 27.

Bird, Kai & Martin J. Sherwin 2006. *American Prometheus: The triumph and tragedy of J. Robert Oppenheimer.* New York: Vintage Books.

Blankenbuehler, Paige 2018. Cashing in on Standing Rock: How *Veterans Stand* squandered $1.4 million raised around the #NoDAPL. *HighCountryNews*, April 13.

Bonnes, Stephanie 2017. The bureaucratic harassment of U.S. servicewomen. *Gender & Society 31*: 804–829.

Bonnes, Stephanie 2020. Service-women's responses to sexual harassment: The importance of identity work and masculinity in a gendered organization. *Violence Against Women 26*: 1656–1680.

Branson-Potts, Hailey & Matt Stiles 2020. Thousands take to the streets for All Black Lives Matter rally. *Los Angeles Times*, June 15.

Cabosky, Joseph 2019. If you're using "Millennial" as a meaningful measurement, you should probably stop. *The Conversation*, October 22.

Carruthers, Charlene A. 2018. *Unapologetic: A Black, queer, and feminist mandate for radical movements.* Boston: Beacon Press.

Cheng, Sealing 2013. *On the move for love: Migrant entertainers in the U.S. military in South Korea.* Philadelphia: University of Pennsylvania Press.

Cohn, Carol 2004. Feminist peacemaking. *Women's Review of Books 21* (5): 8–9.

Cohn, Carol 2013. Women and wars: Toward a conceptual framework. Pp. 1–35 in Carol Cohn, ed., *Women and wars.* Malden, MA: Polity.

Cohn, Carol & Ruth Jacobson 2013. Women and political activism in the face of war and militarization. Pp. 102–123 in Carol Cohn, ed., *Women and wars.* Malden, MA: Polity.

Collins, Patricia Hill 1986. Learning from the outsider within: The sociological significance of Black feminist thought. *Social Problems 33*: 14–32.

Collins, Patricia Hill 1990. *Black feminist thought: Knowledge, consciousness and the politics of empowerment.* New York: Routledge.

Collins, Patricia Hill 2013. The ethos of violence. Pp. 187–197 in Patricia Hill Collins, ed., *On intellectual activism.* Philadelphia: Temple University Press.

Collins, Patricia Hill 2019. *Intersectionality as critical social theory.* Durham & London: Duke University Press.

Combahee River Collective 1977. A Black feminist statement. Pp. 13–22 in Gloria Hull & Patricia Bell Scott, eds., *All the women are White, all the Blacks are men, but some of us are brave: Black women's studies.* New York: Feminist Press.

Connell, Catherine 2017. Now that we can ask and tell: The social movement legacy of the DADT repeal. *Sociology Compass 11*: 1–13.

Conroy, Pat 1976. *The great Santini.* New York: Random House.

Conroy, Pat 1980. *The lords of discipline.* New York: Houghton Mifflin.

Cordova, Tina 2018. Tularosa Basin Downwinders. *Atomic Heritage Foundation*, July 31. https://www.atomicheritage.org/history/tularosa-basin-downwinders.

Correales, Robert I. 2008. Don't Ask, Don't Tell: A dying policy on the precipice. *Western Law Review 44*: 413–476.

Crenshaw, Kimberle Williams 1989. Demarginalizing the intersection of race and sex: A Black feminist critique of antidiscrimination doctrine, feminist theory and antiracist politics. *University of Chicago Legal Forum 140*: 139–167.

Crenshaw, Kimberle Williams 1991. Mapping the margins: Intersectionality, identity politics and violence against women of color. *Stanford Law Review 43*: 1241–1299.

Crossley, Alison Dahl 2019. Online feminism is just feminism: Offline and online move-ment persistence. Pp. 60–78 in Jo Reger, ed., *Nevertheless, they persisted: Feminisms and continued resistance in the U.S. women's movement*. New York & London: Routledge.

Davis, Angela Y. 2016. *Freedom is a constant struggle: Ferguson, Palestine, and the founda-tions of a movement*. Chicago, IL: Haymarket Books.

Davis, Angela Y. 2020. Abolition feminism. Pp. 203–216 in Brenna Bhandar & Rafeef Ziadah, eds., *Revolutionary feminisms*. London & New York: Verso.

DeBarros, Brittany Ramos 2014. Four things you may not know about veterans. *Living Cities*, November 11. https://www.livingcities.org/blog/719-four-things-you-may-not-know-about-veterans.

DeBarros, Brittany Ramos 2015. One female veteran's experience: And other #Goodreads about the state of America's veterans. *Living Cities*, November 13. https://www.livingcities.org/blog/986-one-female-veteran-s-experience-and-other-goodreads-about-the-state-of-america-s-veterans.

DeBarros, Brittany Ramos 2019. An open letter on the systemic mistreatment of womxn of color in social justice spaces. *Time's Up Common Defense*, February 5. https://me-dium.com/timesupprogressives/times-up-common-defense-3a0e0795cf0d.

De Beauvoir, Simone 2015 (1948). *The ethics of ambiguity*. New York: Philosophical Library.

DeLargy, Pamela 2013. Sexual violence and women's health in war. Pp. 54–79 in Carol Cohn, ed., *Women and wars*. Malden, MA: Polity.

del Duca, Rosa 2019. *Breaking cadence: One woman's war against the war*. Portland, OR: Ooligan Press.

DiAngelo, Robin 2018. *White fragility: Why it's so hard for White people to talk about racism*. Boston: Beacon Press.

Dill, Bonnie Thornton & Ruth Enid Zambrana 2009. *Emerging intersections: Race, class, and gender in theory, policy, and practice*. New Brunswick, NJ: Rutgers University Press.

Driskill, Qwo-Li 2016. *Asegi stories: Cherokee queer and two-spirit memory*. Tucson: University of Arizona Press.

Eager, Paige Whaley 2014. *Waging gendered wars: U.S. military women in Afghanistan and Iraq*. London: Routledge.

Echols, Alice 2019 (1989) *Daring to be bad: Radical feminism in America, 1967–1975*. Minneapolis: University of Minnesota Press.

Egnell, Robert & Mayesha Alam 2019. *Gender and women in the military: Setting the stage*. Pp. 1–21 in Robert Egnell & Mayesha Alam, eds., Women and gender perspectives in the military: An international comparison. Washington, DC: Georgetown University Press.

Egnell, Robert & Mayesha Alam, eds. 2019. *Women and gender perspectives in the mili-tary: An international comparison*. Washington, DC: Georgetown University Press.

Ehrenreich, Barbara & Dierdre English 2005 (1978). *For her own good: Two centuries of experts' advice to women*. New York: Anchor Books.

Ehrenreich, Barbara & Dierdre English 2010. *Witches, midwives and nurses: A history of women healers* (2nd ed.). New York: The Feminist Press at CUNY.

Enloe, Cynthia 1988. *Does khaki become you? The militarization of women's lives*. London: Harper Collins.

Enloe, Cynthia 1989. *Bananas, beaches and bases: Making feminist sense of international politics*. Berkeley: University of California Press.

Enloe, Cynthia 2000. *Maneuvers: The international politics of militarizing women's lives.* Berkeley: University of California Press.

Enloe, Cynthia 2004. *The curious feminist: Searching for women in a new age of empire.* Berkeley: University of California Press.

Estes, Nick 2019. *Our history is the future: Standing Rock versus the Dakota Access Pipeline, and the long tradition of Indigenous resistance.* London & New York: Verso.

Ferguson, Ann Arnett 2000. *Bad boys: Public schools and the making of Black masculinity.* Ann Arbor: University of Michigan Press.

Fields, Liz 2016. Veterans brought cameras, but also "complete chaos" to Standing Rock. *Vice News*, December 9.

Fisher, Dana R. 2019. *American resistance: From the Women's March to the Blue Wave.* New York: Columbia University Press.

Flores, David 2016. From prowar soldier to antiwar activist: Change and continuity in the narratives of political conversion among Iraq War Veterans. *Symbolic Interaction* (1533-8665 online).

Freire, Paulo 1970. *Pedagogy of the oppressed.* New York: Herder & Herder.

Glenn, Evelyn Nakano 2009. *Unequal freedoms: How race and gender shaped American citizenship.* Cambridge, MA: Harvard University Press.

Gonzalez, Roberto J., Hugh Gusterson, & Gustaaf Houtman, eds. 2019. *Militarization: A reader.* Durham & London: Duke University Press.

Goode, William J. 1980. Why men resist. *Dissent* (Spring).

Gordon, Suzanne 2018. *Wounds of war: How the VA delivers health, healing, and hope to the nation's veterans.* Ithaca & London: ILR Press.

Greenwood, Ronni Michelle 2008. Intersectional political consciousness: Appreciation for intergroup differences and solidarity in diverse groups. *Psychology of Women Quarterly 32*: 36–47.

Grosse, Corrie 2019. Ecofeminism and climate justice. Pp. 185–203 in Jo Reger, ed., *Nevertheless, they persisted: Feminisms and continued resistance in the U.S. women's movement.* New York & London: Routledge.

Groves, Julian McAllister 1997. *Hearts and minds: The controversy over laboratory animals.* Philadelphia: Temple University Press.

Gusterson, Hugh 2016. *Drone: Remote control warfare.* Cambridge, MA: MIT Press.

Gutmann, Matthew & Catherine Lutz 2010. *Breaking ranks: Iraq veterans speak out against the war.* Berkeley: University of California Press.

Hancock, Ange-Marie 2016. *Intersectionality: An intellectual history.* New York: Oxford University Press.

Harris, Adrienne 1989. Bringing Artemis to life: A plea for militance and aggression in feminist peace politics. Pp. 93–113 in Adrienne Harris & Ynestra King, eds., *Rocking the ship of state: Toward a feminist peace politics.* Boulder, San Francisco, & London: Westview Press.

Heitt, Alex 2019. Albuquerque Proud Boys demonstration generates resistance. *DailyLobo.com*, September 16.

Henry, Nicola 2016. Theorizing wartime rape: Deconstructing gender, sexuality and violence. *Gender & Society 10*: 44–56.

Hondagneu-Sotelo, Pierrette 2008. *God's heart has no borders: How religious activists are working for immigrant rights.* Berkeley: University of California Press.

Hondagneu-Sotelo, Pierrette, Genelle Gaudinez, Hector Lara, & Billie C. Ortiz 2004. "There's a spirit that transcends the border": Faith, ritual, and postnational protest at the U.S.–Mexico Border. *Sociological Perspectives 47*: 133–159.

hooks, bell 1984. *Feminist theory: From margin to center*. Boston: South End Press.

Hunt, Sarah 2016. *An introduction to the health of Two-Spirit people: Historical, contemporary and emergent issues*. Prince George, BC: National Collaborating Centre for Aboriginal Health.

Hunt, Theresa Ann 2018. A movement divided: Slutwalks, protest repertoires and the privilege of nudity. *Social Movements Studies 17*: 541–557.

Hurwitz, Heather McKee 2019. #FemGA #SayHerName #NotHereForBoys: Feminist spillover in U.S. social movements, 2011–2016. Pp. 115–132 in Jo Reger, ed., *Nevertheless, they persisted: Feminisms and continued resistance in the U.S. women's movement*. New York & London: Routledge.

Hutto, Jonathan W. 2008. *Antiwar soldier: How to dissent within the ranks of the military*. New York: Nation Books.

Jackson, Catrice M. 2017. *White spaces missing faces: Why women of color don't trust White women*. Omaha, NE: Catriciology Enterprises.

Jasper, James M. 2004. A strategic approach to collective action: Looking for agency in social movement choices. *Mobilization: An international journal 9*: 1–16.

Jasper, James M. 2018. *The emotions of protest*. Chicago & London: University of Chicago Press.

Jasper, James M., Michael P. Young, & Elke Zuern 2020. *Public characters: The politics of reputation and blame*. New York: Oxford University Press.

Johnson, Akemi 2019. *Night in the American village: Women in the shadow of U.S. military bases in Okinawa*. New York & London: The New Press.

Kanter, Rosabeth Moss 1977. *Men and women of the corporation*. New York: Basic.

Kendi, Ibram X. 2019. *How to be an antiracist*. New York: One World.

Kirk, Gwyn 1989. Our Greenham Common: Feminism and nonviolence. Pp 115–130 in Adrienne Harris & Ynestra King, eds., *Rocking the ship of state: Toward a feminist peace politics*. Boulder, San Francisco, & London: Westview Press.

Klein, Naomi 2007. *The shock doctrine: The rise of disaster capitalism*. New York: Metropolitan Books.

LaDuke, Winona with Sean Aaron Cruz 2012. *The militarization of Indian country*. East Lansing: Makwa Enewed.

Lane, Rebecca, Erika Tarzi, Kristen Post, & Eric Gauldin 2018. Marine corps organizational research project report to Personnel Studies and Oversight Office: Marines' perspectives on various aspects of marine corps organizational culture. USCM Center For Advanced Operational Culture Learning, EDCOM, March 30.

Le Guin, Ursula K. 1973. The ones who walk away from Omelas. In Robert Silverberg, ed., *New Dimensions 3*. Garden City, NY: Nelson Doubleday/SFBC.

Leise, Kylea Laina 2019. Childbirth in the context of conflict in Afghanistan. Pp. 41–56 in Catherine Lutz & Andrea Mazzarino, eds., *War and health: The medical consequences of the wars in Iraq and Afghanistan*. New York: New York University Press.

Leitz, Lisa 2014. *Fighting for peace: Veterans and military families in the anti–Iraq War movement*. Minneapolis: University of Minnesota Press.

Leslie, Kristen J. 2019. Betrayal by friendly fire. Pp. 245–255 in Robert Emmet Meagher & Douglas A. Pryer, eds., *War and moral injury: A reader*. Eugene, OR: Cascade Books.

Levine, Philippa 2004. "A multitude of unchaste women": Prostitution in the British Empire. *Journal of Women's History 15* (4): 159–163.

Linton, Rhoda 1989. Seneca women's peace camp: Shapes of things to come. Pp. 239–261 in Adrienne Harris & Ynestra King, eds., *Rocking the ship of state: Toward a feminist peace politics*. Boulder, San Francisco, & London: Westview Press.

Litz, Brett T. & Patricia K. Kerig 2019. Introduction to the special issue on moral injury: Conceptual challenges, methodological issues, and clinical applications. *Journal of Traumatic Stress 32*: 341–349.

Litz, Brett T., N. Stein, E. Delaney, L. Lebowitz, W. P. Nash, C. Silva, & S. Maguen 2009. Moral injury and moral repair in war veterans: A preliminary model and intervention strategy. *Clinical Psychology Review 29*: 695–706.

Lorde, Audre 1981. The uses of anger: Women responding to racism. Keynote address, National Women's Studies Association, Storrs, CT, June.

Lorde, Audre 2007 (1984). Age, race, class, and sex: Women redefining difference. Pp. 114–123 in Audre Lorde, ed., *Sister outsider: Essays and speeches*. Berkeley: Crossing Press.

Lucas, Carrie L., Julie A. Cederbaum, Sarah Kintzle, & Carl Andrew Castro 2019. An examination of stalking experiences during military service among female and male veterans and associations with PTSD and depression. *Journal of Interpersonal Violence*, pp. 1–22.

Luna, Zakiya 2016. "Truly a women of color organization": Negotiating sameness and difference in the pursuit of intersectionality. *Gender & Society 30*: 769–790.

Lutz, Catherine 2002. Making war at home in the United States: Militarization and the current crisis. *American Anthropologist 104* (3): 723–735.

Lutz, Catherine 2004. Living room terrorists: Rates of domestic violence are three to five times higher among military couples than among civilian ones. *Women's Review of Books 21* (5): 17–18.

Lyman, Peter 1981. The politics of anger: On silence, ressentiment, and political speech. *Socialist Review 57*: 55–74.

Manning, Lory 2004. Military women: Who they are, what they do, and why it matters. *Women's Review of Books 21* (5): 7–8.

Marx, Karl 1988 (1844). *Economic and philosophic manuscripts of 1844*. Buffalo, NY: Prometheus Books.

Mazzarino, Andrea, Marcial C. Inhorn, & Catherine Lutz 2019. The health consequences of war. Pp. 1–37 in Catherine Lutz & Andrea Mazzarino, eds., *War and health: The medical consequences of the wars in Iraq and Afghanistan*. New York: New York University Press.

McCall, Leslie 2005. The complexity of intersectionality. *Signs: Journal of Women in Culture and Society 30*: 1771–1800.

McGuffey, C. Shawn 2018. Intersectionality, cognition, disclosure and Black LGBT views on civil rights and marriage equality. *Du Bois Review 15*: 441–465.

Meagher, Robert Emmet & Douglas A. Pryer, eds. *War and moral injury: A reader*. Eugene, OR: Cascade Books.

Mele, Christopher 2016. Veterans to serve as "human shields" for Dakota Access Pipeline protestors. *The New York Times*, December 14.

Messner, Michael A. 2005. The triad of violence in men's sports. In E. Buchwald, P. R. Fletcher & M. Roth, eds., *Transforming a rape culture*. Minneapolis: Milkweed Editions.

Messner, Michael A. 2014. Can locker room rape culture be prevented? *Contexts: Understanding People in Their Social Worlds* (Spring).

Messner, Michael A. 2015. Intersectionality without women of color? *Girl w/Pen*, June 19. https://thesocietypages.org/girlwpen/2015/06/19/intersectionality-without-women-of-color/.

Messner, Michael A. 2016. Bad men, good men, bystanders: Who is the rapist? *Gender & Society 30*: 57–66.

Messner, Michael A. 2019. *Guys like me: Five wars, five veterans for peace.* New Brunswick, NJ: Rutgers University Press.

Messner, Michael A., Max A. Greenberg, & Tal Peretz 2015. *Some men: Feminist allies and the movement to end violence against women.* New York: Oxford University Press.

Meyer, David S. and Nancy Whittier. 1994. Social movement spillover. *Social Problems 41* (2): 277.

Milkman, Ruth 2014. Millennial movements: Occupy Wall Street and the Dreamers. *Dissent 61* (3): 55–59.

Milkman, Ruth 2017. A new political generation: Millennials and the post-2008 wave of protest. *American Sociological Review 82* (1):1–31.

Mills, C. Wright 1959. *The sociological imagination.* New York: Oxford University Press.

Misra, Joya 2018. Categories, structures, and intersectional theory. Pp. 111–130 in James W. Messerschmidt, Patricia Yancey Martin, Michael A. Messner, & Raewyn Connell, eds., *Gender reckonings: New social theory and research.* New York: New York University Press.

Montez de Oca, Jeffrey 2012. White domestic goddess on a postmodern plantation: Charity and commodity racism in *The Blind Side. Sociology of Sport Journal 29*: 131–151.

Moore, Brenda L. 1996. From underrepresentation to overrepresentation: African American women. Pp. 115–135 in Judith Hicks Stiehm, ed., *It's our military too!: Women and the U.S. military.* Philadelphia: Temple University Press.

Moore, Mignon R. 2012. Intersectionality and the study of Black, sexual minority women. *Gender & Society 26*: 33–39.

Moraga, Cherrie & Gloria Anzaldua 1981. *This bridge called my back: Writings by radical women of color.* Watertown, MA: Persephone Press.

Morgan, Robin, ed. 1970. *Sisterhood is powerful: An anthology of writings from the women's liberation movement.* New York: Vintage Books.

Mosse, George L. 2000. Shell shock as a social disease. *Journal of Contemporary History 35*: 101–108.

Nadal, Kevin L., Katie E. Griffin, Yinglee Wong, Sahran Hamit, & Morgan Rasmus 2014. The impact of racial microaggressions on mental health: Counseling implications for clients of color. *Journal of Counseling and Development 92*: 57–66.

Nolan, Tom 2020. Militarization has fostered a policing culture that sets up protestors as "the enemy." *The Conversation*, June 2.

Omolade, Barbara 1989. We speak for the planet. Pp. 171–189 in Adrienne Harris & Ynestra King, eds., *Rocking the ship of state: Toward a feminist peace politics.* Boulder, San Francisco, & London: Westview Press.

Opperman, Brenda 2019. Women and gender in the U.S. military: A slow process of integration. Pp. 113–140 in Robert Egnell & Mayesha Alam, eds., *Women and gender perspectives in the military: An international comparison.* Washington, DC: Georgetown University Press.

Parvini, Sarah 2020. To reform or reconstruct?: Young Black activists, challenging "respectability politics" of their elders, give voice to a new movement for social change. *Los Angeles Times*, June 15.

Patton, Eileen & Kim Parker 2011. Women in the U.S. military: Growing share, distinctive profile. *PEW Social and demographic trends.* PEW Research Center.

Peach, Lucinda Joy 1996. Gender ideology and the ethics of women in combat. Pp. 156–194 in Judith Hicks Stiehm, ed., *It's our military too! Women and the U.S. military.* Philadelphia: Temple University Press.

Pilisuk, Mark & Ines-Lena Mahr 2015. Psychology and the prevention of war trauma. *Journal for Social Action in Counseling and Psychology 7*: 122–142.

Powell, Wilson. M., ed. 2008. *The democratization of Veterans For Peace, 1995–2007*. Veterans for Peace.

Raven-Roberts, Angela. 2013. Women and the political economy of war. Pp. 36–53 in Carol Cohn, ed., *Women and wars*. Malden, MA: Polity.

Reger, Jo 2019. The making of a march: Identity, intersectionality and diffusion of U.S. feminism. Pp. 2–22 in Jo Reger, ed., *Nevertheless, they persisted: Feminisms and continued resistance in the U.S. women's movement*. New York & London: Routledge.

Reeves, Connie L. 1996. The military women's vanguard: Nurses. In Judith Hicks Stiehm, ed., *Our military too! Women and the U.S. military*. Philadelphia: Temple University Press.

Reichbach, Alex 2019. Alt-right groups rally, outnumbered by counterprotestors. *NMPoliticalReport*, September 15.

Renteln, Alison Dundes 2020. A political analysis of sexual violence in the International Criminal Court. Pp. 102–125 in Julie Fraser & Brionne McGonigle Leyh, eds., *Intersections of law and culture at the International Criminal Court*. Cheltenham, UK: Edward Elgar Publisher.

Reynolds, George M. & Amanda Shendruk 2018. Demographics of the U.S. military. Council on Foreign Relations, April 24.

Ríos, Monisha 2019. The glue is still drying. Pp. 83–94 in Robert Emmet Meagher & Douglas A. Pryer, eds., *War and moral injury: A reader*. Eugene, OR: Cascade Books.

Roth, Benita 2010. *Separate roads to feminism: Black, Chicana, and White feminist movements in America's second wave*. Cambridge: Cambridge University Press.

Ruddick, Sarah 1989. Mothers and men's wars. Pp. 75–92 in Adrienne Harris & Ynestra King, eds., *Rocking the ship of state: Toward a feminist peace politics*. Boulder, San Francisco, & London: Westview Press.

Rupp, Leila J. & Verta Taylor 1987. *Survival in the doldrums: The American women's movement, 1945–the 1960s*. New York & Oxford: Oxford University Press.

Sasson-Levey, Orna, Yagil Levy, & Edna Lomsky-Feder 2011. Women breaking the silence: Military service, gender and antiwar protest. *Gender & Society 25*: 740–763.

Schrader, Benjamin 2019. The affect of veteran activism. *Critical Military Studies 5*: 63–77.

Shay, Jonathan 1994. *Achilles in Vietnam: Combat trauma and the undoing of character*. New York: Scribner.

Shay, Jonathan 2014. Moral injury. *Psychoanalytic Psychology 31*: 182–191.

Shilts, Randy 1993. *Conduct unbecoming: Gays and lesbians in the U.S. military*. New York: St. Martin's Press.

Silliman, Stephen W. 2008. The "Old West" in the Middle East: U.S. military metaphors in real and imagined Indian country. *American Anthropologist 110*: 237–247.

Smith, Dorothy E. 1989. *The everyday world as problematic: A feminist sociology*. Boston: Northeastern University Press.

Staggenborg, Suzanne & Verta Taylor 2005. What ever happened to the women's movement? *Mobilization: An International Journal 10*: 37–52.

Staples, Robert 1979. The myth of the Black macho: A response to angry Black feminists. *The Black Scholar 10*.

Stiehm, Judith Hicks 1996. Just the facts, ma'am. Pp. 60–70 in Judith Hicks Stiehm, ed., *It's our military too! Women and the U.S. military*. Philadelphia: Temple University Press.

Street, Amy E., Dwayne Vogt, & Lissa Dutra 2009. A new generation of women veterans: Stressors faced by women deployed to Iraq and Afghanistan. *Clinical Psychology Review 29*: 685–694.

Suarez, Fatima 2019. Identifying with inclusivity: Intersectional Chicana feminisms. Pp. 25–42 in Jo Reger, ed., *Nevertheless, they persisted: Feminisms and continued resistance in the U.S. women's movement.* New York & London: Routledge.

Sweet, Paige L. 2019. The sociology of gaslighting. *American Sociological Review 84*: 851–875.

Swerdlow, Amy 1989. Pure milk, not poison: Women strike for peace and the Test Ban Treaty of 1963. Pp. 225–237 in Adrienne Harris & Ynestra King, eds., *Rocking the ship of state: Toward a feminist peace politics.* Boulder, San Francisco, & London: Westview Press.

Taylor, Verta 1989. Social movement continuity: The women's movement in abeyance. *American Sociological Review 54*: 761–775.

Taylor, Verta 1996. *Rock-a-by baby: Feminism, self-help, and postpartum depression.* New York: Routledge.

Taylor, Verta & Leila J. Rupp 2002. Loving internationalism: The emotion culture of transnational women's organizations, 1888-1945. *Mobilization: An International Journal 7*: 125–144.

Terriquez, Veronica 2015. Intersectional mobilization, social movement spillover, and queer youth leadership in the immigrant rights movement. *Social Problems 62* (3): 343–362.

Terriquez, Veronica 2015. Training young activists: Grassroots organizing and youths' civic and political trajectories. *Sociological Perspectives 58*: 223–242.

Theidon, Kimberly 2007. Gender in transition: Common sense, women and war. *Journal of Human Rights 6*: 453–478.

Tickner, J. Ann 2002. Feminist perspectives on 9/11. *International Studies Perspectives 3*: 333–350.

Tirman, John 2011. *The deaths of others: The fate of civilians in America's wars.* New York: Oxford University Press.

Tuck, Eve & K. Wayne Yang 2012. Decolonization is not a metaphor. *Decolonization: Indigeneity, Education & Society 1*: 1–40.

van Gelder, Sarah 2016. Veteran Wesley Clark Jr: Why I knelt before Standing Rock elders and asked for forgiveness. *YES! Magazine*, December 22.

Walker, Alice 1979. Coming apart. Pp. 41–53 in Alice Walker, ed., *You can't keep a good woman down: Short stories.* Orlando: Harcourt, Inc.

Wallace, Michelle 1979. *Black macho and the myth of the super-woman.* New York: Warner Books.

Walls, Melissa L., John Gonzalez, Tanya Gladney, & Emily Onello 2015. Unconscious biases: Racial microaggressions in American Indian healthcare. *Journal of the American Board of Family Medicine 28*: 231–239.

Walters, K. L., T. Evans-Campbell, J. Wimomi, T. Ronquillo, & R. Bhuyan 2006. "My spirit in my heart": Identity experiences and challenges among American Indian two-spirited women. *Journal of Lesbian Studies 10*: 125–149.

Ward, Brian 2020. From the Green New Deal to the Red Deal. *The Red Nation*, April 10. https://therednation.org/2020/04/10/from-the-green-new-deal-to-the-red-deal/.

Wingfield, Adia Harvey 2007. The modern mammy and the angry Black man: African-American professionals' experiences with gendered racism in the workplace. *Race, Gender and Class: 14*: 196–212.

Wingfield, Adia Harvey 2010. Are some emotions marked "White Only?": Racialized feeling rules in professional workplaces. *Social Problems 57*: 251–266.

Wingfield, Adia Harvey, & Renee Skeete 2014. Maintaining hierarchies in predominantly White organizations: A theory of racial tasks. *American Behavioral Scientist 58*: 274–287.

Wittner, Lawrence S. 1969. *Rebels against war: The American peace movement, 1941–1960.* New York & London: Columbia University Press.

Wojnicka, Katarzyna 2019. Social movements and intersectionality: The case of migrants' social activism. Pp. 168–184 in S. Zajak & S. Haunss, eds., *Social stratification and social movements*. London: Routledge.

Yazdiha, Hajir 2020. An intersectional theory of strategic action: Socially located memories, cultural knowledge, and Muslim rights. *Mobilization: An International Journal 25: 475–492.*

Zambrana, Ruth Enid 2018. *Toxic ivory towers: The consequences of work stress on underrepresented minority faculty.* New Brunswick, NJ: Rutgers University Press.

Index

For the benefit of digital users, indexed terms that span two pages (e.g., 52–53) may, on occasion, appear on only one of those pages.

Note: Figures are indicated by *f* following the page number

Trump, Donald, 8–9, 87, 88–90, 97–98,
103, 125–26
Tuck, Eve, 102–3

Unapologetic (Carruthers), 53
unconscious biases, 66
United Nations Security Council
(UNSC), 2
uranium miners, 106
U.S. Air Force, 19–20, 25–34, 77, 139n.16
U.S. Army, 18–25, 77, 80–81, 91, 97, 110,
139n.16
U.S. Army Reserve, 32, 44
U.S. bombings of Hiroshima and
Nagasaki, 106–7
U.S. border policies. *See* social injustices of
U.S. border policies
U.S. Customs and Border Protection
(CBP), 79, 81
U.S. Marine Corps, 3, 18–20, 25, 38–43,
62, 63, 97, 139n.16
U.S. Navy, 19, 26, 35, 39, 40, 122–23,
139n.16

Veteran Artists, 95, 126
veterans. *See also* About Face; Iraq
Veterans Against the War; Veterans
For Peace
activism by, xiv
acute stress disorder by, 37
adjustment disorder in, 37
alcohol use by, 27, 28–29, 31–32, 39
anger of, 24, 28, 31–32, 37
anti-war veterans, 11–12, 25, 41–43, 75
behavioral issues of, 23–24
drug use by, 23–24, 28–29, 32, 33, 135
employment problems of, 28–29
gendered racism against women, 55, 67,
68, 133
homelessness of, 29, 33
internalized trauma of, 3
LGBTQ2S people, 1–2
military trauma in, 20–29, 133, 135
PTSD in, 3, 37, 47, 69–70, 95, 146n.15
queer-identified persons, xiv–xv, 11–12,
19–20, 31–32, 44, 121
younger generation of, 114–
28, 133–34

Veterans Administration (VA) health care
system, 3
Veterans For Peace (VFP)
anti-militarism focus of, 82
climate activism, 103–9, 105*f*
coalition-building and, 79–89, 80*f*
critical analysis of militarism, 91–93
critical examination of, 52–56
decolonization movements, 102–6,
107, 110–11
ebb and flow of, 129–32
gendered double-standard of
anger, 69–70
internal sexism and racism, 15, 74–75
intersectionality and, 1–2, 5–6, 9–13
intersectional praxis in social
movements, 114–28
leadership of, 64
male hostility in meetings, 71–72, 73–74
men's elevator banter, 50–51
microaggressions in, 67
"performative" commitment to
diversity, 73–74
personal narratives, 14–15, 16–17, 33–
34, 38, 43, 48
sexual and gender justice, 93–96
Standing Rock activism, 96–103
tokenism and, 56–62
younger generation of veterans, 114–28
Veterans Organizing Institute, 79–80
veterans' peace movements
"abeyance strategies" by, 129, 149–
50n.4, 154n.12
critical examination of VFP, 52–56
cross-generational analysis of, 112–14
emotions and, 69–72
gaslighting in, 68, 72–76
gender and, 4–6
intersectionality and, 8–13
leadership in, 62–65
marginalization in, 52, 56, 57, 60, 62, 66,
73, 75–76, 114–15
microaggressions in, 65–68, 72–76
misogyny in, 55, 57, 95, 124
overview of, 1–2
queer-identified persons and, 52, 55,
57, 72, 75–76, 94–95, 108, 114, 118,
126–27, 133–34